AI
Self-Driving Cars
Consonance

Practical Advances in
Artificial Intelligence and Machine Learning

Dr. Lance B. Eliot, MBA, PhD

Disclaimer: This book is presented solely for educational and entertainment purposes. The author and publisher are not offering it as legal, accounting, or other professional services advice. The author and publisher make no representations or warranties of any kind and assume no liabilities of any kind with respect to the accuracy or completeness of the contents and specifically disclaim any implied warranties of merchantability or fitness of use for a particular purpose. Neither the author nor the publisher shall be held liable or responsible to any person or entity with respect to any loss or incidental or consequential damages caused, or alleged to have been caused, directly or indirectly, by the information or programs contained herein. Every company is different and the advice and strategies contained herein may not be suitable for your situation.

 First Edition.

ISBN: 978-1-73-460169-5

DEDICATION

To my incredible daughter, Lauren, and my incredible son, Michael.

Forest fortuna adiuvat (from the Latin; good fortune favors the brave).

CONTENTS

ACKNOWLEDGMENTS

I have been the beneficiary of advice and counsel by many friends, colleagues, family, investors, and many others. I want to thank everyone that has aided me throughout my career. I write from the heart and the head, having experienced first-hand what it means to have others around you that support you during the good times and the tough times.

To Warren Bennis, one of my doctoral advisors and ultimately a colleague, I offer my deepest thanks and appreciation, especially for his calm and insightful wisdom and support.

To Mark Stevens and his generous efforts toward funding and supporting the USC Stevens Center for Innovation.

To Lloyd Greif and the USC Lloyd Greif Center for Entrepreneurial Studies for their ongoing encouragement of founders and entrepreneurs.

To Peter Drucker, William Wang, Aaron Levie, Peter Kim, Jon Kraft, Cindy Crawford, Jenny Ming, Steve Milligan, Chis Underwood, Frank Gehry, Buzz Aldrin, Steve Forbes, Bill Thompson, Dave Dillon, Alan Fuerstman, Larry Ellison, Jim Sinegal, John Sperling, Mark Stevenson, Anand Nallathambi, Thomas Barrack, Jr., and many other innovators and leaders that I have met and gained mightily from doing so.

Thanks to Ed Trainor, Kevin Anderson, James Hickey, Wendell Jones, Ken Harris, DuWayne Peterson, Mike Brown, Jim Thornton, Abhi Beniwal, Al Biland, John Nomura, Eliot Weinman, John Desmond, and many others for their unwavering support during my career.

And most of all thanks as always to Lauren and Michael, for their ongoing support and for having seen me writing and heard much of this material during the many months involved in writing it. To their patience and willingness to listen.

INTRODUCTION

This is a book that provides the newest innovations and the latest Artificial Intelligence (AI) advances about the emerging nature of AI-based autonomous self-driving driverless cars. Via recent advances in Artificial Intelligence (AI) and Machine Learning (ML), we are nearing the day when vehicles can control themselves and will not require and nor rely upon human intervention to perform their driving tasks (or, that allow for human intervention, but only *require* human intervention in very limited ways).

Similar to my other related books, which I describe in a moment and list the chapters in the Appendix A of this book, I am particularly focused on those advances that pertain to self-driving cars. The phrase "autonomous vehicles" is often used to refer to any kind of vehicle, whether it is ground-based or in the air or sea, and whether it is a cargo hauling trailer truck or a conventional passenger car. Though the aspects described in this book are certainly applicable to all kinds of autonomous vehicles, I am focused more so here on cars.

Indeed, I am especially known for my role in aiding the advancement of self-driving cars, serving currently as the Executive Director of the Cybernetic AI Self-Driving Cars Institute. In addition to writing software, designing and developing systems and software for self-driving cars, I also speak and write quite a bit about the topic. This book is a collection of some of my more advanced essays. For those of you that might have seen my essays posted elsewhere, I have updated them and integrated them into this book as one handy cohesive package.

You might be interested in companion books that I have written that provide additional key innovations and fundamentals about self-driving cars. Those books are entitled **"Introduction to Driverless Self-Driving Cars,"** "**Advances in AI and Autonomous Vehicles: Cybernetic Self-Driving Cars,**" "**Self-Driving Cars: "The Mother of All AI Projects," "Innovation and Thought Leadership on Self-Driving Driverless Cars," "New Advances in AI Autonomous Driverless Self-Driving Cars," "Autonomous Vehicle Driverless Self-Driving Cars and Artificial Intelligence," "Transformative Artificial Intelligence Driverless Self-Driving Cars," "Disruptive Artificial Intelligence and Driverless Self-Driving Cars,** and **"State-of-the-Art AI Driverless Self-Driving Cars,"** and **"Top Trends in AI Self-Driving Cars,"** and **"AI Innovations and Self-Driving Cars," "Crucial Advances for AI**

Driverless Cars," "Sociotechnical Insights and AI Driverless Cars," "Pioneering Advances for AI Driverless Cars" and **"Leading Edge Trends for AI Driverless Cars," "The Cutting Edge of AI Autonomous Cars"** and **"The Next Wave of AI Self-Driving Cars"** and **"Revolutionary Innovations of AI Self-Driving Cars,"** and **"AI Self-Driving Cars Breakthroughs," "Trailblazing Trends for AI Self-Driving Cars," "Ingenious Strides for AI Driverless Cars," "AI Self-Driving Cars Inventiveness," "Visionary Secrets of AI Driverless Cars," "Spearheading AI Self-Driving Cars," "Spurring AI Self-Driving Cars," "Avant-Garde AI Driverless Cars," "AI Self-Driving Cars Evolvement," "AI Driverless Cars Chrysalis," "Boosting AI Autonomous Cars," "AI Self-Driving Cars Trendsetting," "AI Autonomous Cars Forefront, "AI Autonomous Cars Emergence," "AI Autonomous Cars Progress," "AI Self-Driving Cars Prognosis," "AI Self-Driving Cars Momentum," "AI Self-Driving Cars Headway," "AI Self-Driving Cars Vicissitude," "AI Self-Driving Cars Autonomy," "AI Driverless Cars Transmutation," "AI Driverless Cars Potentiality," "AI Driverless Cars Realities," "AI Self-Driving Cars Materiality, "AI Self-Driving Cars Accordance," "AI Self-Driving Cars Equanimity," "AI Self-Driving Cars Divulgement," "AI Self-Driving Cars Consonance"** (they are available on Amazon).

For this book, I am going to borrow my introduction from those companion books, since it does a good job of laying out the landscape of self-driving cars and my overall viewpoints on the topic.

INTRODUCTION TO SELF-DRIVING CARS

This is a book about self-driving cars. Someday in the future, we'll all have self-driving cars and this book will perhaps seem antiquated, but right now, we are at the forefront of the self-driving car wave. Daily news bombards us with flashes of new announcements by one car maker or another and leaves the impression that within the next few weeks or maybe months that the self-driving car will be here. A casual non-technical reader would assume from these news flashes that in we must be on the cusp of a true self-driving car.

We are still quite a distance from having a true self-driving car. A true self-driving car is akin to a moonshot. In the same manner that getting us to the moon was an incredible feat, likewise, is achieving a true self-driving car. Anybody that suggests or even brashly states that the true self-driving car is nearly here should be viewed with great skepticism. Indeed, you'll see that I often tend to use the word "hogwash" or "crock" when I assess much of the decidedly ***fake news*** about self-driving cars.

Indeed, I've been writing a popular blog post about self-driving cars and hitting hard on those that try to wave their hands and pretend that we are on the imminent verge of true self-driving cars. For many years, I've been known as the AI Insider. Besides writing about AI, I also develop AI software. I do what I describe. It also gives me insights into what others that are doing AI are really doing versus what it is said they are doing.

Many faithful readers had asked me to pull together my insightful short essays and put them into another book, which you are now holding.

For those of you that have been reading my essays over the years, this collection not only puts them together into one handy package, I also updated the essays and added new material. For those of you that are new to the topic of self-driving cars and AI, I hope you find these essays approachable and informative. I also tend to have a writing style with a bit of a voice, and so you'll see that I am times have a wry sense of humor and poke at conformity.

As a former professor and founder of an AI research lab, I for many years wrote in the formal language of academic writing. I published in referred journals and served as an editor for several AI journals. This writing here is not of the nature, and I have adopted a different and more informal style for these essays. That being said, I also do mention from time-to-time more rigorous material on AI and encourage you all to dig into those deeper and more formal materials if so interested.

I am also an AI practitioner. This means that I write AI software for a living. Currently, I head-up the Cybernetics Self-Driving Car Institute, where we are developing AI software for self-driving cars.

For those of you that are reading this book and have a penchant for writing code, you might consider taking a look at the open source code available for self-driving cars. This is a handy place to start learning how to develop AI for self-driving cars. There are also many new educational courses spring forth. There is a growing body of those wanting to learn about and develop self-driving cars, and a growing body of colleges, labs, and other avenues by which you can learn about self-driving cars.

This book will provide a foundation of aspects that I think will get you ready for those kinds of more advanced training opportunities. If you've already taken those classes, you'll likely find these essays especially interesting as they offer a perspective that I am betting few other instructors or faculty offered to you. These are challenging essays that ask you to think beyond the conventional about self-driving cars.

THE MOTHER OF ALL AI PROJECTS

In June 2017, Apple CEO Tim Cook came out and finally admitted that Apple has been working on a self-driving car. As you'll see in my essays, Apple was enmeshed in secrecy about their self-driving car efforts. We have only been able to read the tea leaves and guess at what Apple has been up to. The notion of an iCar has been floating for quite a while, and self-driving engineers and researchers have been signing tight-lipped Non-Disclosure Agreements (NDA's) to work on projects at Apple that were as shrouded in mystery as any military invasion plans might be.

Tim Cook said something that many others in the Artificial Intelligence (AI) field have been saying, namely, the creation of a self-driving car has got to be the mother of all AI projects. In other words, it is in fact a tremendous moonshot for AI. If a self-driving car can be crafted and the AI works as we hope, it means that we have made incredible strides with AI and that therefore it opens many other worlds of potential breakthrough accomplishments that AI can solve.

Is this hyperbole? Am I just trying to make AI seem like a miracle worker and so provide self-aggrandizing statements for those of us writing the AI software for self-driving cars? No, it is not hyperbole. Developing a true self-driving car is really, really, really hard to do. Let me take a moment to explain why. As a side note, I realize that the Apple CEO is known for at times uttering hyperbole, and he had previously said for example that the year 2012 was "the mother of all years," and he had said that the release of iOS 10 was "the mother of all releases" – all of which does suggest he likes to use the handy "mother of" expression. But, I assure you, in terms of true self-driving cars, he has hit the nail on the head. For sure.

When you think about a moonshot and how we got to the moon, there are some identifiable characteristics and those same aspects can be applied to creating a true self-driving car. You'll notice that I keep putting the word "true" in front of the self-driving car expression. I do so because as per my essay about the various levels of self-driving cars, there are some self-driving cars that are only somewhat of a self-driving car. The somewhat versions are ones that require a human driver to be ready to intervene. In my view, that's not a true self-driving car. A true self-driving car is one that requires no human driver intervention at all. It is a car that can entirely undertake via automation the driving task without any human driver needed. This is the essence of what is known as a Level 5 self-driving car. We are currently at the Level 2 and Level 3 mark, and not yet at Level 5.

Getting to the moon involved aspects such as having big stretch goals, incremental progress, experimentation, innovation, and so on. Let's review how this applied to the moonshot of the bygone era, and how it applies to the self-driving car moonshot of today.

Big Stretch Goal

Trying to take a human and deliver the human to the moon, and bring them back, safely, was an extremely large stretch goal at the time. No one knew whether it could be done. The technology wasn't available yet. The cost was huge. The determination would need to be fierce. Etc. To reach a Level 5 self-driving car is going to be the same. It is a big stretch goal. We can readily get to the Level 3, and we are able to see the Level 4 just up ahead, but a Level 5 is still an unknown as to if it is doable. It should eventually be doable and in the same way that we thought we'd eventually get to the moon, but when it will occur is a different story.

Incremental Progress

Getting to the moon did not happen overnight in one fell swoop. It took years and years of incremental progress to get there. Likewise, for self-driving cars. Google has famously been striving to get to the Level 5, and pretty much been willing to forgo dealing with the intervening levels, but most of the other self-driving car makers are doing the incremental route. Let's get a good Level 2 and a somewhat Level 3 going. Then, let's improve the Level 3 and get a somewhat Level 4 going. Then, let's improve the Level 4 and finally arrive at a Level 5. This seems to be the prevalent way that we are going to achieve the true self-driving car.

Experimentation

You likely know that there were various experiments involved in perfecting the approach and technology to get to the moon. As per making incremental progress, we first tried to see if we could get a rocket to go into space and safety return, then put a monkey in there, then with a human, then we went all the way to the moon but didn't land, and finally we arrived at the mission that actually landed on the moon.

Self-driving cars are the same way. We are doing simulations of self-driving cars. We do testing of self-driving cars on private land under controlled situations.

We do testing of self-driving cars on public roadways, often having to meet regulatory requirements including for example having an engineer or equivalent in the car to take over the controls if needed. And so on. Experiments big and small are needed to figure out what works and what doesn't.

Innovation

There are already some advances in AI that are allowing us to progress toward self-driving cars. We are going to need even more advances. Innovation in all aspects of technology are going to be required to achieve a true self-driving car. By no means do we already have everything in-hand that we need to get there. Expect new inventions and new approaches, new algorithms, etc.

Setbacks

Most of the pundits are avoiding talking about potential setbacks in the progress toward self-driving cars. Getting to the moon involved many setbacks, some of which you never have heard of and were buried at the time so as to not dampen enthusiasm and funding for getting to the moon. A recurring theme in many of my included essays is that there are going to be setbacks as we try to arrive at a true self-driving car. Take a deep breath and be ready. I just hope the setbacks don't completely stop progress. I am sure that it will cause progress to alter in a manner that we've not yet seen in the self-driving car field. I liken the self-driving car of today to the excitement everyone had for Uber when it first got going. Today, we have a different view of Uber and with each passing day there are more regulations to the ride sharing business and more concerns raised. The darling child only stays a darling until finally that child acts up. It will happen the same with self-driving cars.

SELF-DRIVING CARS CHALLENGES

But what exactly makes things so hard to have a true self-driving car, you might be asking. You have seen cruise control for years and years. You've lately seen cars that can do parallel parking. You've seen YouTube videos of Tesla drivers that put their hands out the window as their car zooms along the highway, and seen to therefore be in a self-driving car. Aren't we just needing to put a few more sensors onto a car and then we'll have in-hand a true self-driving car? Nope.

Consider for a moment the nature of the driving task. We don't just let anyone at any age drive a car. Worldwide, most countries won't license a driver until the age of 18, though many do allow a learner's permit at the age of 15 or 16. Some suggest that a younger age would be physically too small to reach the controls of the car. Though this might be the case, we could easily adjust the controls to allow for younger aged and thus smaller stature. It's not their physical size that matters. It's their cognitive development that matters.

To drive a car, you need to be able to reason about the car, what the car can and cannot do. You need to know how to operate the car. You need to know about how other cars on the road drive. You need to know what is allowed in driving such as speed limits and driving within marked lanes. You need to be able to react to situations and be able to avoid getting into accidents. You need to ascertain when to hit your brakes, when to steer clear of a pedestrian, and how to keep from ramming that motorcyclist that just cut you off.

Many of us had taken courses on driving. We studied about driving and took driver training. We had to take a test and pass it to be able to drive. The point being that though most adults take the driving task for granted, and we often "mindlessly" drive our cars, there is a significant amount of cognitive effort that goes into driving a car. After a while, it becomes second nature. You don't especially think about how you drive, you just do it. But, if you watch a novice driver, say a teenager learning to drive, you suddenly realize that there is a lot more complexity to it than we seem to realize.

Furthermore, driving is a very serious task. I recall when my daughter and son first learned to drive. They are both very conscientious people. They wanted to make sure that whatever they did, they did well, and that they did not harm anyone. Every day, when you get into a car, it is probably around 4,000 pounds of hefty metal and plastics (about two tons), and it is a lethal weapon. Think about it. You drive down the street in an object that weighs two tons and with the engine it can accelerate and ram into anything you want to hit. The damage a car can inflict is very scary. Both my children were surprised that they were being given the right to maneuver this monster of a beast that could cause tremendous harm entirely by merely letting go of the steering wheel for a moment or taking your eyes off the road.

In fact, in the United States alone there are about 30,000 deaths per year by auto accidents, which is around 100 per day. Given that there are about 263 million cars in the United States, I am actually more amazed that the number of fatalities is not a lot higher.

During my morning commute, I look at all the thousands of cars on the freeway around me, and I think that if all of them decided to go zombie and drive in a crazy maniac way, there would be many people dead. Somehow, incredibly, each day, most people drive relatively safely. To me, that's a miracle right there. Getting millions and millions of people to be safe and sane when behind the wheel of a two-ton mobile object, it's a feat that we as a society should admire with pride.

So, hopefully you are in agreement that the driving task requires a great deal of cognition. You don't' need to be especially smart to drive a car, and we've done quite a bit to make car driving viable for even the average dolt. There isn't an IQ test that you need to take to drive a car. If you can read and write, and pass a test, you pretty much can legally drive a car. There are of course some that drive a car and are not legally permitted to do so, plus there are private areas such as farms where drivers are young, but for public roadways in the United States, you can be generally of average intelligence (or less) and be able to legally drive.

This though makes it seem like the cognitive effort must not be much. If the cognitive effort was truly hard, wouldn't we only have Einstein's that could drive a car? We have made sure to keep the driving task as simple as we can, by making the controls easy and relatively standardized, and by having roads that are relatively standardized, and so on. It is as though Disneyland has put their Autopia into the real-world, by us all as a society agreeing that roads will be a certain way, and we'll all abide by the various rules of driving.

A modest cognitive task by a human is still something that stymies AI. You certainly know that AI has been able to beat chess players and be good at other kinds of games. This type of narrow cognition is not what car driving is about. Car driving is much wider. It requires knowledge about the world, which a chess playing AI system does not need to know. The cognitive aspects of driving are on the one hand seemingly simple, but at the same time require layer upon layer of knowledge about cars, people, roads, rules, and a myriad of other "common sense" aspects. We don't have any AI systems today that have that same kind of breadth and depth of awareness and knowledge.

As revealed in my essays, the self-driving car of today is using trickery to do particular tasks. It is all very narrow in operation. Plus, it currently assumes that a human driver is ready to intervene. It is like a child that we have taught to stack blocks, but we are needed to be right there in case the child stacks them too high and they begin to fall over.

AI of today is brittle, it is narrow, and it does not approach the cognitive abilities of humans. This is why the true self-driving car is somewhere out in the future.

Another aspect to the driving task is that it is not solely a mind exercise. You do need to use your senses to drive. You use your eyes as vision sensors to see the road ahead. You vision capability is like a streaming video, which your brain needs to continually analyze as you drive. Where is the road? Is there a pedestrian in the way? Is there another car ahead of you? Your senses are relying a flood of info to your brain. Self-driving cars are trying to do the same, by using cameras, radar, ultrasound, and lasers. This is an attempt at mimicking how humans have senses and sensory apparatus.

Thus, the driving task is mental and physical. You use your senses, you use your arms and legs to manipulate the controls of the car, and you use your brain to assess the sensory info and direct your limbs to act upon the controls of the car. This all happens instantly. If you've ever perhaps gotten something in your eye and only had one eye available to drive with, you suddenly realize how dependent upon vision you are. If you have a broken foot with a cast, you suddenly realize how hard it is to control the brake pedal and the accelerator. If you've taken medication and your brain is maybe sluggish, you suddenly realize how much mental strain is required to drive a car.

An AI system that plays chess only needs to be focused on playing chess. The physical aspects aren't important because usually a human moves the chess pieces or the chessboard is shown on an electronic display. Using AI for a more life-and-death task such as analyzing MRI images of patients, this again does not require physical capabilities and instead is done by examining images of bits.

Driving a car is a true life-and-death task. It is a use of AI that can easily and at any moment produce death. For those colleagues of mine that are developing this AI, as am I, we need to keep in mind the somber aspects of this. We are producing software that will have in its virtual hands the lives of the occupants of the car, and the lives of those in other nearby cars, and the lives of nearby pedestrians, etc. Chess is not usually a life-or-death matter.

Driving is all around us. Cars are everywhere. Most of today's AI applications involve only a small number of people. Or, they are behind the scenes and we as humans have other recourse if the AI messes up. AI that is driving a car at 80 miles per hour on a highway had better not mess up. The consequences are grave.

Multiply this by the number of cars, if we could put magically self-driving into every car in the USA, we'd have AI running in the 263 million cars. That's a lot of AI spread around. This is AI on a massive scale that we are not doing today and that offers both promise and potential peril.

There are some that want AI for self-driving cars because they envision a world without any car accidents. They envision a world in which there is no car congestion and all cars cooperate with each other. These are wonderful utopian visions.

They are also very misleading. The adoption of self-driving cars is going to be incremental and not overnight. We cannot economically just junk all existing cars. Nor are we going to be able to affordably retrofit existing cars. It is more likely that self-driving cars will be built into new cars and that over many years of gradual replacement of existing cars that we'll see the mix of self-driving cars become substantial in the real-world.

In these essays, I have tried to offer technological insights without being overly technical in my description, and also blended the business, societal, and economic aspects too. Technologists need to consider the non-technological impacts of what they do. Non-technologists should be aware of what is being developed.

We all need to work together to collectively be prepared for the enormous disruption and transformative aspects of true self-driving cars.

WHAT THIS BOOK PROVIDES

What does this book provide to you? It introduces many of the key elements about self-driving cars and does so with an AI based perspective. I weave together technical and non-technical aspects, readily going from being concerned about the cognitive capabilities of the driving task and how the technology is embodying this into self-driving cars, and in the next breath I discuss the societal and economic aspects.

They are all intertwined because that's the way reality is. You cannot separate out the technology per se, and instead must consider it within the milieu of what is being invented and innovated, and do so with a mindset towards the contemporary mores and culture that shape what we are doing and what we hope to do.

WHY THIS BOOK

I wrote this book to try and bring to the public view many aspects about self-driving cars that nobody seems to be discussing.

For business leaders that are either involved in making self-driving cars or that are going to leverage self-driving cars, I hope that this book will enlighten you as to the risks involved and ways in which you should be strategizing about how to deal with those risks.

For entrepreneurs, startups and other businesses that want to enter into the self-driving car market that is emerging, I hope this book sparks your interest in doing so, and provides some sense of what might be prudent to pursue.

For researchers that study self-driving cars, I hope this book spurs your interest in the risks and safety issues of self-driving cars, and also nudges you toward conducting research on those aspects.

For students in computer science or related disciplines, I hope this book will provide you with interesting and new ideas and material, for which you might conduct research or provide some career direction insights for you.

For AI companies and high-tech companies pursuing self-driving cars, this book will hopefully broaden your view beyond just the mere coding and development needed to make self-driving cars.

For all readers, I hope that you will find the material in this book to be stimulating. Some of it will be repetitive of things you already know. But I am pretty sure that you'll also find various eureka moments whereby you'll discover a new technique or approach that you had not earlier thought of. I am also betting that there will be material that forces you to rethink some of your current practices.

I am not saying you will suddenly have an epiphany and change what you are doing. I do think though that you will reconsider or perhaps revisit what you are doing.

For anyone choosing to use this book for teaching purposes, please take a look at my suggestions for doing so, as described in the Appendix. I have found the material handy in courses that I have taught, and likewise other faculty have told me that they have found the material handy, in some cases as extended readings and in other instances as a core part of their course (depending on the nature of the class).

In my writing for this book, I have tried carefully to blend both the practitioner and the academic styles of writing.

It is not as abstract as is typical academic journal writing, but at the same time offers depth by going into the nuances and trade-offs of various practices.

The word "deep" is in vogue today, meaning getting deeply into a subject or topic, and so is the word "unpack" which means to tease out the underlying aspects of a subject or topic. I have sought to offer material that addresses an issue or topic by going relatively deeply into it and make sure that it is well unpacked.

In any book about AI, it is difficult to use our everyday words without having some of them be misinterpreted. Specifically, it is easy to anthropomorphize AI. When I say that an AI system "knows" something, I do not want you to construe that the AI system has sentience and "knows" in the same way that humans do. They aren't that way, as yet. I have tried to use quotes around such words from time-to-time to emphasize that the words I am using should not be misinterpreted to ascribe true human intelligence to the AI systems that we know of today. If I used quotes around all such words, the book would be very difficult to read, and so I am doing so judiciously. Please keep that in mind as you read the material, thanks.

Some of the material is time-based in terms of covering underway activities, and though some of it might decay, nonetheless I believe you'll find the material useful and informative.

COMPANION BOOKS BY DR. ELIOT

1. **"Introduction to Driverless Self-Driving Cars"** by Dr. Lance Eliot
2. **"Innovation and Thought Leadership on Self-Driving Driverless Cars"**
3. **"Advances in AI and Autonomous Vehicles: Cybernetic Self-Driving Cars"**
4. **"Self-Driving Cars: The Mother of All AI Projects"** by Dr. Lance Eliot
5. **"New Advances in AI Autonomous Driverless Self-Driving Cars"**
6. **"Autonomous Vehicle Driverless Self-Driving Cars and Artificial Intelligence"** by Dr. Lance Eliot and Michael B. Eliot
7. **"Transformative Artificial Intelligence Driverless Self-Driving Cars"**
8. **"Disruptive Artificial Intelligence and Driverless Self-Driving Cars"**
9. "State-of-the-Art AI Driverless Self-Driving Cars" by Dr. Lance Eliot
10. "**Top Trends in AI Self-Driving Cars**" by Dr. Lance Eliot
11. **"AI Innovations and Self-Driving Cars"** by Dr. Lance Eliot
12. **"Crucial Advances for AI Driverless Cars"** by Dr. Lance Eliot
13. **"Sociotechnical Insights and AI Driverless Cars"** by Dr. Lance Eliot.
14. **"Pioneering Advances for AI Driverless Cars"** by Dr. Lance Eliot
15. **"Leading Edge Trends for AI Driverless Cars"** by Dr. Lance Eliot
16. **"The Cutting Edge of AI Autonomous Cars"** by Dr. Lance Eliot
17. **"The Next Wave of AI Self-Driving Cars"** by Dr. Lance Eliot
18. **"Revolutionary Innovations of AI Driverless Cars"** by Dr. Lance Eliot
19. **"AI Self-Driving Cars Breakthroughs"** by Dr. Lance Eliot
20. **"Trailblazing Trends for AI Self-Driving Cars"** by Dr. Lance Eliot
21. **"Ingenious Strides for AI Driverless Cars"** by Dr. Lance Eliot
22. **"AI Self-Driving Cars Inventiveness"** by Dr. Lance Eliot
23. **"Visionary Secrets of AI Driverless Cars"** by Dr. Lance Eliot
24. **"Spearheading AI Self-Driving Cars"** by Dr. Lance Eliot
25. **"Spurring AI Self-Driving Cars"** by Dr. Lance Eliot
26. **"Avant-Garde AI Driverless Cars"** by Dr. Lance Eliot
27. **"AI Self-Driving Cars Evolvement"** by Dr. Lance Eliot
28. **"AI Driverless Cars Chrysalis"** by Dr. Lance Eliot
29. **"Boosting AI Autonomous Cars"** by Dr. Lance Eliot
30. **"AI Self-Driving Cars Trendsetting"** by Dr. Lance Eliot
31. **"AI Autonomous Cars Forefront"** by Dr. Lance Eliot
32. **"AI Autonomous Cars Emergence"** by Dr. Lance Eliot
33. **"AI Autonomous Cars Progress"** by Dr. Lance Eliot
34. **"AI Self-Driving Cars Prognosis"** by Dr. Lance Eliot
35. **"AI Self-Driving Cars Momentum"** by Dr. Lance Eliot
36. **"AI Self-Driving Cars Headway"** by Dr. Lance Eliot
37. **"AI Self-Driving Cars Vicissitude"** by Dr. Lance Eliot
38. **"AI Self-Driving Cars Autonomy"** by Dr. Lance Eliot
39. **"AI Driverless Cars Transmutation"** by Dr. Lance Eliot
40. **"AI Driverless Cars Potentiality"** by Dr. Lance Eliot
41. **"AI Driverless Cars Realities"** by Dr. Lance Eliot
42. **"AI Self-Driving Cars Materiality"** by Dr. Lance Eliot
43. **"AI Self-Driving Cars Accordance"** by Dr. Lance Eliot
44. **"AI Self-Driving Cars Equanimity"** by Dr. Lance Eliot
45. **"AI Self-Driving Cars Divulgement"** by Dr. Lance Eliot
46. **"AI Self-Driving Cars Consonance" by Dr. Lance Eliot**

These books are available on Amazon and at other major global booksellers.

CHAPTER 1

ELIOT FRAMEWORK FOR AI SELF-DRIVING CARS

CHAPTER 1

ELIOT FRAMEWORK FOR AI SELF-DRIVING CARS

This chapter is a core foundational aspect for understanding AI self-driving cars and I have used this same chapter in several of my other books to introduce the reader to essential elements of this field. Once you've read this chapter, you'll be prepared to read the rest of the material since the foundational essence of the components of autonomous AI driverless self-driving cars will have been established for you.

When I give presentations about self-driving cars and teach classes on the topic, I have found it helpful to provide a framework around which the various key elements of self-driving cars can be understood and organized (see diagram at the end of this chapter). The framework needs to be simple enough to convey the overarching elements, but at the same time not so simple that it belies the true complexity of self-driving cars. As such, I am going to describe the framework here and try to offer in a thousand words (or more!) what the framework diagram itself intends to portray.

The core elements on the diagram are numbered for ease of reference. The numbering does not suggest any kind of prioritization of the elements. Each element is crucial. Each element has a purpose, and otherwise would not be included in the framework. For some self-driving cars, a particular element might be more important or somehow distinguished in comparison to other self-driving cars.

You could even use the framework to rate a particular self-driving car, doing so by gauging how well it performs in each of the elements of the framework. I will describe each of the elements, one at a time. After doing so, I'll discuss aspects that illustrate how the elements interact and perform during the overall effort of a self-driving car.

At the AI Self-Driving Car Institute, we use the framework to keep track of what we are working on, and how we are developing software that fills in what is needed to achieve Level 5 self-driving cars.

D-01: Sensor Capture

Let's start with the one element that often gets the most attention in the press about self-driving cars, namely, the sensory devices for a self-driving car.

On the framework, the box labeled as D-01 indicates "Sensor Capture" and refers to the processes of the self-driving car that involve collecting data from the myriad of sensors that are used for a self-driving car. The types of devices typically involved are listed, such as the use of mono cameras, stereo cameras, LIDAR devices, radar systems, ultrasonic devices, GPS, IMU, and so on.

These devices are tasked with obtaining data about the status of the self-driving car and the world around it. Some of the devices are continually providing updates, while others of the devices await an indication by the self-driving car that the device is supposed to collect data. The data might be first transformed in some fashion by the device itself, or it might instead be fed directly into the sensor capture as raw data. At that point, it might be up to the sensor capture processes to do transformations on the data. This all varies depending upon the nature of the devices being used and how the devices were designed and developed.

D-02: Sensor Fusion

Imagine that your eyeballs receive visual images, your nose receives odors, your ears receive sounds, and in essence each of your distinct sensory devices is getting some form of input. The input befits the nature of the device. Likewise, for a self-driving car, the cameras provide visual images, the radar returns radar reflections, and so on. Each device provides the data as befits what the device does.

At some point, using the analogy to humans, you need to merge together what your eyes see, what your nose smells, what your ears hear, and piece it all together into a larger sense of what the world is all about and what is happening around you. Sensor fusion is the action of taking the singular aspects from each of the devices and putting them together into a larger puzzle.

Sensor fusion is a tough task. There are some devices that might not be working at the time of the sensor capture. Or, there might some devices that are unable to report well what they have detected. Again, using a human analogy, suppose you are in a dark room and so your eyes cannot see much. At that point, you might need to rely more so on your ears and what you hear. The same is true for a self-driving car. If the cameras are obscured due to snow and sleet, it might be that the radar can provide a greater indication of what the external conditions consist of.

In the case of a self-driving car, there can be a plethora of such sensory devices. Each is reporting what it can. Each might have its difficulties. Each might have its limitations, such as how far ahead it can detect an object. All of these limitations need to be considered during the sensor fusion task.

D-03: Virtual World Model

For humans, we presumably keep in our minds a model of the world around us when we are driving a car. In your mind, you know that the car is going at say 60 miles per hour and that you are on a freeway.

You have a model in your mind that your car is surrounded by other cars, and that there are lanes to the freeway. Your model is not only based on what you can see, hear, etc., but also what you know about the nature of the world. You know that at any moment that car ahead of you can smash on its brakes, or the car behind you can ram into your car, or that the truck in the next lane might swerve into your lane.

The AI of the self-driving car needs to have a virtual world model, which it then keeps updated with whatever it is receiving from the sensor fusion, which received its input from the sensor capture and the sensory devices.

D-04: System Action Plan

By having a virtual world model, the AI of the self-driving car is able to keep track of where the car is and what is happening around the car. In addition, the AI needs to determine what to do next. Should the self-driving car hit its brakes? Should the self-driving car stay in its lane or swerve into the lane to the left? Should the self-driving car accelerate or slow down?

A system action plan needs to be prepared by the AI of the self-driving car. The action plan specifies what actions should be taken. The actions need to pertain to the status of the virtual world model. Plus, the actions need to be realizable.

This realizability means that the AI cannot just assert that the self-driving car should suddenly sprout wings and fly. Instead, the AI must be bound by whatever the self-driving car can actually do, such as coming to a halt in a distance of X feet at a speed of Y miles per hour, rather than perhaps asserting that the self-driving car come to a halt in 0 feet as though it could instantaneously come to a stop while it is in motion.

D-05: Controls Activation

The system action plan is implemented by activating the controls of the car to act according to what the plan stipulates.

This might mean that the accelerator control is commanded to increase the speed of the car. Or, the steering control is commanded to turn the steering wheel 30 degrees to the left or right.

One question arises as to whether or not the controls respond as they are commanded to do. In other words, suppose the AI has commanded the accelerator to increase, but for some reason it does not do so. Or, maybe it tries to do so, but the speed of the car does not increase. The controls activation feeds back into the virtual world model, and simultaneously the virtual world model is getting updated from the sensors, the sensor capture, and the sensor fusion. This allows the AI to ascertain what has taken place as a result of the controls being commanded to take some kind of action.

By the way, please keep in mind that though the diagram seems to have a linear progression to it, the reality is that these are all aspects of the self-driving car that are happening in parallel and simultaneously. The sensors are capturing data, meanwhile the sensor fusion is taking place, meanwhile the virtual model is being updated, meanwhile the system action plan is being formulated and reformulated, meanwhile the controls are being activated.

This is the same as a human being that is driving a car. They are eyeballing the road, meanwhile they are fusing in their mind the sights, sounds, etc., meanwhile their mind is updating their model of the world around them, meanwhile they are formulating an action plan of what to do, and meanwhile they are pushing their foot onto the pedals and steering the car. In the normal course of driving a car, you are doing all of these at once. I mention this so that when you look at the diagram, you will think of the boxes as processes that are all happening at the same time, and not as though only one happens and then the next.

They are shown diagrammatically in a simplistic manner to help comprehend what is taking place. You though should also realize that they are working in parallel and simultaneous with each other. This is a tough aspect in that the inter-element communications involve latency and other aspects that must be taken into account.

There can be delays in one element updating and then sharing its latest status with other elements.

D-06: Automobile & CAN

Contemporary cars use various automotive electronics and a Controller Area Network (CAN) to serve as the components that underlie the driving aspects of a car. There are Electronic Control Units (ECU's) which control subsystems of the car, such as the engine, the brakes, the doors, the windows, and so on.

The elements D-01, D-02, D-03, D-04, D-05 are layered on top of the D-06, and must be aware of the nature of what the D-06 is able to do and not do.

D-07: In-Car Commands

Humans are going to be occupants in self-driving cars. In a Level 5 self-driving car, there must be some form of communication that takes place between the humans and the self-driving car. For example, I go into a self-driving car and tell it that I want to be driven over to Disneyland, and along the way I want to stop at In-and-Out Burger. The self-driving car now parses what I've said and tries to then establish a means to carry out my wishes.

In-car commands can happen at any time during a driving journey. Though my example was about an in-car command when I first got into my self-driving car, it could be that while the self-driving car is carrying out the journey that I change my mind. Perhaps after getting stuck in traffic, I tell the self-driving car to forget about getting the burgers and just head straight over to the theme park. The self-driving car needs to be alert to in-car commands throughout the journey.

D-08: V2X Communications

We will ultimately have self-driving cars communicating with each other, doing so via V2V (Vehicle-to-Vehicle) communications.

We will also have self-driving cars that communicate with the roadways and other aspects of the transportation infrastructure, doing so via V2I (Vehicle-to-Infrastructure).

The variety of ways in which a self-driving car will be communicating with other cars and infrastructure is being called V2X, whereby the letter X means whatever else we identify as something that a car should or would want to communicate with. The V2X communications will be taking place simultaneous with everything else on the diagram, and those other elements will need to incorporate whatever it gleans from those V2X communications.

D-09: Deep Learning

The use of Deep Learning permeates all other aspects of the self-driving car. The AI of the self-driving car will be using deep learning to do a better job at the systems action plan, and at the control's activation, and at the sensor fusion, and so on.

Currently, the use of artificial neural networks is the most prevalent form of deep learning. Based on large swaths of data, the neural networks attempt to "learn" from the data and therefore direct the efforts of the self-driving car accordingly.

D-10: Tactical AI

Tactical AI is the element of dealing with the moment-to-moment driving of the self-driving car. Is the self-driving car staying in its lane of the freeway? Is the car responding appropriately to the controls commands? Are the sensory devices working?

For human drivers, the tactical equivalent can be seen when you watch a novice driver such as a teenager that is first driving. They are focused on the mechanics of the driving task, keeping their eye on the road while also trying to properly control the car.

D-11: Strategic AI

The Strategic AI aspects of a self-driving car are dealing with the larger picture of what the self-driving car is trying to do. If I had asked that the self-driving car take me to Disneyland, there is an overall journey map that needs to be kept and maintained.

There is an interaction between the Strategic AI and the Tactical AI. The Strategic AI is wanting to keep on the mission of the driving, while the Tactical AI is focused on the particulars underway in the driving effort. If the Tactical AI seems to wander away from the overarching mission, the Strategic AI wants to see why and get things back on track. If the Tactical AI realizes that there is something amiss on the self-driving car, it needs to alert the Strategic AI accordingly and have an adjustment to the overarching mission that is underway.

D-12: Self-Aware AI

Very few of the self-driving cars being developed are including a Self-Aware AI element, which we at the Cybernetic Self-Driving Car Institute believe is crucial to Level 5 self-driving cars.

The Self-Aware AI element is intended to watch over itself, in the sense that the AI is making sure that the AI is working as intended. Suppose you had a human driving a car, and they were starting to drive erratically. Hopefully, their own self-awareness would make them realize they themselves are driving poorly, such as perhaps starting to fall asleep after having been driving for hours on end. If you had a passenger in the car, they might be able to alert the driver if the driver is starting to do something amiss.

This is exactly what the Self-Aware AI element tries to do, it becomes the overseer of the AI, and tries to detect when the AI has become faulty or confused, and then find ways to overcome the issue.

D-13: Economic

The economic aspects of a self-driving car are not per se a technology aspect of a self-driving car, but the economics do indeed impact the nature of a self-driving car. For example, the cost of outfitting a self-driving car with every kind of possible sensory device is prohibitive, and so choices need to be made about which devices are used. And, for those sensory devices chosen, whether they would have a full set of features or a more limited set of features.

We are going to have self-driving cars that are at the low-end of a consumer cost point, and others at the high-end of a consumer cost point. You cannot expect that the self-driving car at the low-end is going to be as robust as the one at the high-end. I realize that many of the self-driving car pundits are acting as though all self-driving cars will be the same, but they won't be. Just like anything else, we are going to have self-driving cars that have a range of capabilities. Some will be better than others. Some will be safer than others. This is the way of the real-world, and so we need to be thinking about the economics aspects when considering the nature of self-driving cars.

D-14: Societal

This component encompasses the societal aspects of AI which also impacts the technology of self-driving cars. For example, the famous Trolley Problem involves what choices should a self-driving car make when faced with life-and-death matters. If the self-driving car is about to either hit a child standing in the roadway, or instead ram into a tree at the side of the road and possibly kill the humans in the self-driving car, which choice should be made?

We need to keep in mind the societal aspects will underlie the AI of the self-driving car. Whether we are aware of it explicitly or not, the AI will have embedded into it various societal assumptions.

D-15: Innovation

I included the notion of innovation into the framework because we can anticipate that whatever a self-driving car consists of, it will continue to be innovated over time. The self-driving cars coming out in the next several years will undoubtedly be different and less innovative than the versions that come out in ten years hence, and so on.

Framework Overall

For those of you that want to learn about self-driving cars, you can potentially pick a particular element and become specialized in that aspect. Some engineers are focusing on the sensory devices. Some engineers focus on the controls activation. And so on. There are specialties in each of the elements.

Researchers are likewise specializing in various aspects. For example, there are researchers that are using Deep Learning to see how best it can be used for sensor fusion. There are other researchers that are using Deep Learning to derive good System Action Plans. Some are studying how to develop AI for the Strategic aspects of the driving task, while others are focused on the Tactical aspects.

A well-prepared all-around software developer that is involved in self-driving cars should be familiar with all of the elements, at least to the degree that they know what each element does. This is important since whatever piece of the pie that the software developer works on, they need to be knowledgeable about what the other elements are doing.

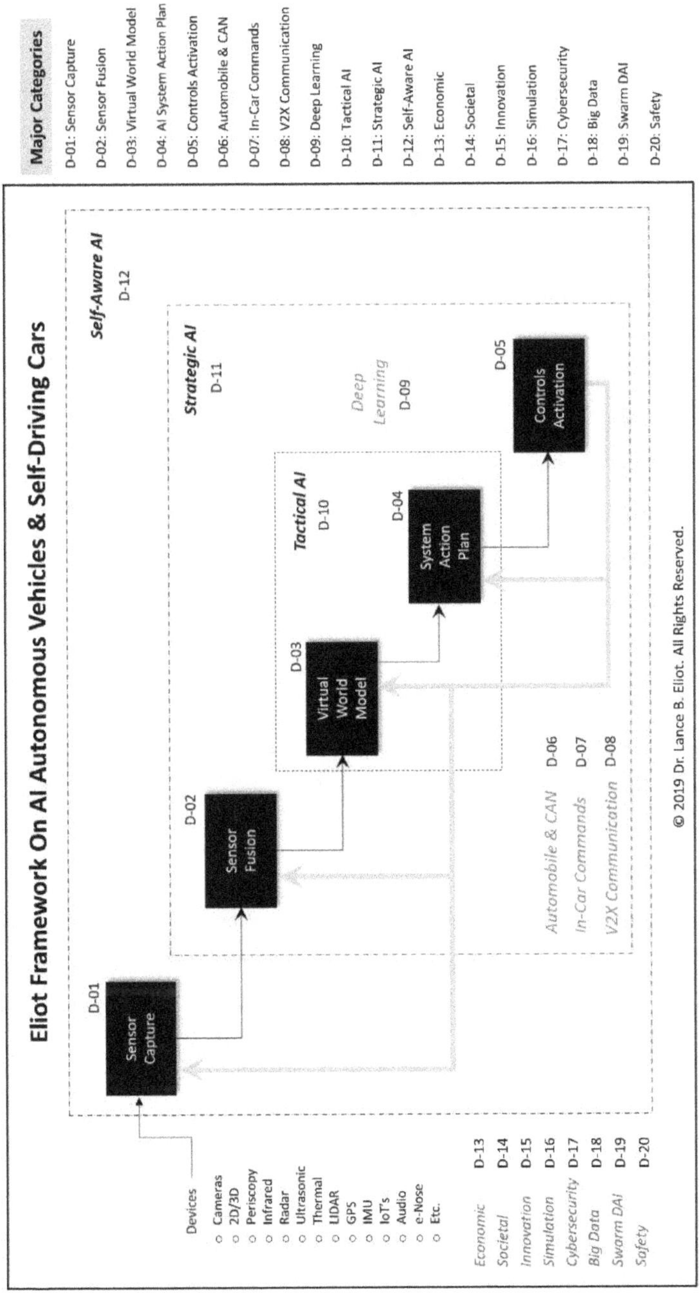
Eliot Framework On AI Autonomous Vehicles & Self-Driving Cars
Major Categories
D-01: Sensor Capture
D-02: Sensor Fusion
D-03: Virtual World Model
D-04: AI System Action Plan
D-05: Controls Activation
D-06: Automobile & CAN
D-07: In-Car Commands
D-08: V2X Communication
D-09: Deep Learning
D-10: Tactical AI
D-11: Strategic AI
D-12: Self-Aware AI
D-13: Economic
D-14: Societal
D-15: Innovation
D-16: Simulation
D-17: Cybersecurity
D-18: Big Data
D-19: Swarm DAI
D-20: Safety
Self-Aware AI
D-12
Strategic AI
D-11
Tactical AI
D-10
Deep Learning
D-09
Sensor Capture
D-01
Sensor Fusion
D-02
Virtual World Model
D-03
System Action Plan
D-04
Controls Activation
D-05
Automobile & CAN D-06
In-Car Commands D-07
V2X Communication D-08
Devices
Cameras
2D/3D
Periscopy
Infrared
Radar
Ultrasonic
Thermal
LIDAR
GPS
IMU
IoT's
Audio
e-Nose
Etc.
Economic D-13
Societal D-14
Innovation D-15
Simulation D-16
Cybersecurity D-17
Big Data D-18
Swarm DAI D-19
Safety D-20
© 2019 Dr. Lance B. Eliot. All Rights Reserved.

CHAPTER 2
BABY YODA ON HOODS AND AI SELF-DRIVING CARS

CHAPTER 2

BABY YODA ON HOODS AND AI SELF-DRIVING CARS

Baby Yoda has taken the world by storm.

Headlines have blared that resistance is futile to defy the allure of Baby Yoda and some exclaim that Baby Yoda managed to break the internet.

Baby Yoda, love you must; meanwhile, Baby Yoda memes are seemingly throughout the universe, or at least universally being shared and adored.

Why do we find ourselves so impulsively agog over the emergence of Baby Yoda?

First, anything associated with Star Wars is obviously going to immediately have a leg up in gleaning widespread attention and interest.

That's a given.

Secondly, by-and-large, anything that has an adorable baby-like look is bound to catch or engage our inner lizard, meaning that we are presumably DNA-ingrained with an autonomic response to having positive feelings toward babies.

Presumably, we are prodded into the ongoing survival and extension of our species by the pre-programmed urge to embrace and care for a baby.

Darwin's theories seem to apply in an overarching way, namely that by having a built-in instinct to gravitate toward a baby and a presumed willingness to aid the baby due to an uncontrollable sense of affection and attraction, we keep ourselves going and repeat our species.

And, yes, you can pretty much say the same about most animals too.

To be clear, I am not suggesting that as humans we are unique in this genetic encoding, only that we perhaps have taken it to a higher art form by the fact that we can create tons of both physical and online realizations, such as memes, posters, pictures, animations, toys, and a slew of irresistible merchandise that triggers our innate reactions to babies.

For those of you that are either tired of the Baby Yoda mania, or that claim you were never attracted to it, to begin with, perhaps you've found a means to counteract your own primordial impulses. If so, either pat yourself on the back, or, on the behalf of Baby Yoda lovers everywhere, get over it and join the club with everyone else.

Third, humans also seem to have a natural affinity for facial recognition, which turns out to be potentially integral to the Baby Yoda phenomena.

Here's what I mean.

In ways that have yet to be fully explained, we have an incredible capacity to scan around ourselves and spot any faces that might be nearby.

Furthermore, once you spot a face, you tend to nearly immediately codify the face into your brain's memory banks.

At some later point in time, you can usually readily identify if you've seen that face before.

Even causal and momentary glances at other people can produce this same amazingly eclectic recollection ability.

If you look around a crowd of strangers and take just a moment to look earnestly at those around you, the odds are that you'll be able to, later on, pick out faces from a line-up, and you would vocally attest to having seen those faces previously.

Don't though interpret this indication to overstate our facial recognition prowess.

It isn't perfect, by any means.

People are notorious for asserting vigorously in courtroom trials that they saw someone, yet the truth might be that they did not.

Sometimes, we catch a glimpse of someone's face and then fill in the rest in our memory banks, falsely so at times, and create a composite that is not the actual person that we saw.

Also, oftentimes people cannot remember when or where they say a particular face. It seems that we can mentally bring forth an image of a face, but it doesn't necessarily come attached with a definitive time stamp, which a picture taken via a good camera might do.

There are lots of other foibles involved in our facial recognition aptitude.

Your memory of someone's face can morph over time, thus, six months later your minds-eye of a previously seen face is no longer what you might have captured earlier. Within your brain, it could be that the nose is reshaped, the hair repositioned, the skin tone altered, and so on.

This could be likened to having your own mental Photoshop that changes the faces that you've seen.

Worse still, you might not realize that you've indeed mentally altered a face. Yes, the person had gray hair and blue eyes, you claim with great conviction, and yet it could be that they had faintly colored hair and brown eyes.

What does this have to do with Baby Yoda?

If you take a studious glance at Baby Yoda, you'll notice that this mankind hand-crafted "baby" has quite large and innocent-looking eyes, the kind that causes us to immediately melt, which happens too when you see a young puppy with big eyes.

That's a smart way to design a baby-like toy or image, doing so in a manner that invokes our facial recognition mental engine and gets us inextricably engaged, whether we wish to do so, or we don't.

Keep looking and you'll also notice that the forehead is placed rather high.

Score another point for baby-dom.

There are somewhat chubby or cute-ish cheeks.

Kaching!

Score another point.

Gaze at the relatively petite nose.

Add it all up into one face, especially a babyface, and its bingo time.

In formal parlance, you have fallen for the standardized infant schema that we seem to be programmed to succumb to.Advertising and marketing have long leveraged this predisposition and likely further reinforced the innate capability, ratcheting up the ingrained part of our psyche to get attention to slick ads and boastful marketing materials, doing so via explicitly or sneakily including babies, and thus make a buck off our unstoppable push-button urges.

Kudos to the Baby Yoda "inventors" that shrewdly enacted their own grand convergence.

The trifecta consists of a lovable looking baby character that is associated with the tremendously popular Star Wars tidal wave and that is crafted well enough to automatically invoke our innate snuggling response (by the way, if they had missed the mark, and if the baby looked askew, we probably wouldn't be talking about the matter, and this latest new creation would have ended up on the junk heap of failed new tricks and toys).

As an aside, in the field of AI and especially robotics, it is well-known that you need to walk a fine line between crafting something that looks human-like and yet doesn't under-step and nor over-step what is portrayed as being humanish.

A robot that looks extremely crude and mechanical is generally okay for humans to see and react to since right away people assess and categorize the robot as not a human and that it is only a robot.

At the other extreme, a robot that looks nearly exactly like a human and if it seemingly acts like a human, we tend to find that acceptable, at least with respect to a willingness to interact with the robot and not instantly recoil at seeing it.

There's a kind of valley in-between those two extremes, whereby there might be a robot that doesn't look fully human and yet it doesn't look fully like a robot per se and sits in a kind of purgatory that's an untoward middle ground.

For most people, they tend to have a sense of repulsion when seeing an in-between style of a robot, whereby the person reacts coldly or negatively to something that is a not-quite-a-robot and yet not-quite-a-human in appearance.

The phrase for those types of muddled middle-ground robots and the reaction to them is known as the "uncanny valley."

Any robot developer worth their salt knows that if their robot lands into the uncanny valley, it means that humans will have a difficult time interacting with the robot because in the back of their human minds the people are having an emotionally adverse reaction to the creation.

In short, a robot that's residing in the uncanny valley is perceived as being eerie and usually unlikable.

Returning to Baby Yoda, if the shape and nature of the facial characteristics were changed to be more human-like, the odds are that it would be Baby Scary rather than the alluring Baby Yoda.

Anyway, as mentioned, the developers got things right and stayed out of the uncanny valley.

Speaking of robots, there's a new kind of robot that is gradually emerging and appearing on our highways, byways, and neighborhood streets.

It's a robot that you've undoubtedly seen in videos and pictures and depending upon where you live might have witnessed this robot going down your street.

I'm referring to self-driving cars.

Most people are shocked to think of a self-driving car as a robot.

Generally, we consider a robot to be something that has mechanical arms, legs, etc.

Well, even though a self-driving car doesn't have mechanized arms, legs, and other human-like robotic appendages, it nonetheless can be classified as a kind of robot.

Here's today's interesting question: *"How are people going to react to the widespread adoption of AI-based true self-driving cars, and can Baby Yoda somehow provide some insightful thoughts about the matter?"*

Yes, Baby Yoda can indeed be a help (thanks, Baby Yoda, thanks for being you!).

Let's unpack the matter and see.

The Levels Of Self-Driving Cars

It is important to clarify what I mean when referring to AI-based true self-driving cars.

True self-driving cars are ones that the AI drives the car entirely on its own and there isn't any human assistance during the driving task.

These driverless vehicles are considered a Level 4 and Level 5, while a car that requires a human driver to co-share the driving effort is usually considered at a Level 2 or Level 3. The cars that co-share the driving task are described as being semi-autonomous, and typically contain a variety of automated add-on's that are referred to as ADAS (Advanced Driver-Assistance Systems).

There is not yet a true self-driving car at Level 5, which we don't yet even know if this will be possible to achieve, and nor how long it will take to get there.

Meanwhile, the Level 4 efforts are gradually trying to get some traction by undergoing very narrow and selective public roadway trials, though there is controversy over whether this testing should be allowed per se (we are all life-or-death guinea pigs in an experiment taking place on our highways and byways, some point out).

Since semi-autonomous cars require a human driver, the adoption of those types of cars won't be markedly different than driving conventional vehicles, so there's not much new per se to cover about them on this topic (though, as you'll see in a moment, the points next made are generally applicable).

For semi-autonomous cars, it is important that the public be forewarned about a disturbing aspect that's been arising lately, namely that in spite of those human drivers that keep posting videos of themselves falling asleep at the wheel of a Level 2 or Level 3 car, we all need to avoid being misled into believing that the driver can take away their attention from the driving task while driving a semi-autonomous car.

You are the responsible party for the driving actions of the vehicle, regardless of how much automation might be tossed into a Level 2 or Level 3.

Self-Driving Cars And Baby Yoda

For Level 4 and Level 5 true self-driving vehicles, there won't be a human driver involved in the driving task.

All occupants will be passengers.

The AI is doing the driving.

How in the heck does Baby Yoda get enmeshed into the topic of self-driving cars?

Lots of ways.

First, one of the looming problems for the widespread acceptance of true self-driving cars involves what I have coined "the head nod" problem.

With conventional cars, there is a human driver.

As a pedestrian, and when trying to cross the street, you usually do a quick look at the driver of the oncoming car.

Ponder these life-or-death questions:

- Does the driver see me?

- Is the driver making eye contact or looking away?

- Will the driver let me cross the street or is the driver intent on proceeding unabated?

- If I make a facial expression or movement that suggests I want to cross the street, will this persuade the driver to slow down and let me cross?

- Has the driver shown a facial expression or movement that indicates that they have granted me to cross, or perhaps have they expressed the opposite and are insisting that I shouldn't cross in front of them?

There is quite a societal dance that occurs in the mere act of crossing the street.

Studies show too that this delicate and somber ballet differs depending upon where you live, what your gender or race is, what the prevailing culture is, and a myriad of other factors are involved.

Recall that I just mentioned that for a true self-driving car there isn't a human driver.

In short, there isn't anyone sitting in the driver's seat.

As such, for pedestrians, you have completely now lost the ability to do a head nod negotiation about crossing the street.

Scarily, some people have "figured out" that they can readily win a game of chicken with some driverless cars, doing so by venturing into the street, dangerously so, and the AI system will come to a halt.

Those impetuous pedestrians are playing a game that is much more hazardous than they realize (it's called pranking, see **my discussion here**).

Yes, in theory, self-driving cars are going to give the right-of-way to pedestrians, but there are limits to this possibility.

If you don't time it just right, the AI system might not be able to stop the car in time to avoid hitting you.

Also, you really have no immediate way to know that the AI system detected you, and thus, you are taking quite a chance by moving into the street.

If the AI hasn't via its cameras, radar, LIDAR, and other sensors yet detected you, it could be that by the time it does, it will be too late and you'll be roadkill (I know that seems harsh, but I hope it wakes-up those idiot daredevils that are pranking or playing games with driverless cars).

How to solve this life-or-death problem that will become increasingly apparent once a sufficient adoption of driverless cars occurs?

Many of the automakers and self-driving tech firms are exploring various means to put some kind of visual display on the exterior front portion of the self-driving car.

For example, maybe put large arrows and a red light that lights up to showcase whether the driverless car is going to come to a stop, and also indicates when it is going to make a left or right turn (this would be in addition to the usual turn-blinkers on a car, positioning the arrows up above the front windshield or increased visibility to pedestrians).

Another tryout involves having the headlights appear to be eyeballs, and those seem to shift left or right in their gaze, suggesting that the AI system has seen you and wants to let you know that you've been seen.

Generally, there are a whole bunch of LED displays and similar devices that researchers are experimenting with, hopeful of landing on just the right way to communicate with pedestrians, and, by the way, also communicate with human drivers in other nearby cars that need to do a similar "head nod" communique with a driverless vehicle.

Will people though pay attention to these visual cues?

Even if they do, it could become something that people gradually take for granted and no longer notice.

For those of you that have lived through the era of the addition of a third brake light on the back of our conventional cars, you probably know that at first implementation the new lights seem to really catch the eye of other drivers.

Gradually, according to most studies, people have acclimated themselves to the third brake light and it has much less of an impact than originally envisioned (I'm not saying it has decayed to having no impact at all, only that it is less pronounced as being noticeable and serving to alert other drivers).

Okay, hold your breath for the next statement.

Are you holding your breath?

Alright, here's a novel idea, namely let's put a Baby Yoda on the hood of every true self-driving car.

Say what?

Your first reaction is that this would certainly be a boon for the Star Wars crew and their Baby Yoda creation. There are about 250+ million conventional cars in the United States alone, and if those are ultimately replaced by self-driving cars (though some believe we won't need as many driverless cars as we have of conventional cars), it would mean that there would be perhaps 250 million Baby Yoda's waving at us each and every day.

That's a lot of Baby Yoda's.

Maybe so, but at least we'd pay attention to self-driving cars.

Imagine a mechanical version of a Baby Yoda moving its head to showcase that it "sees" you on the curb and acknowledges that you are seeking to cross the street.

I ask you this, would you dare to prank Baby Yoda and try to trick the self-driving car into coming to a sudden halt?

Not to a baby, and most certainly not to a Baby Yoda!

Those cute eyes, those puffy cheeks, would incredibly brighten your day and you'd certainly be civil and caring for all those driverless cars coming down the street again and again (we might end up with worse congestion in some areas, due to roving driverless cars, see **my analysis here**).

Well, in case some of you are wondering if I've lost my mind, I admittedly am bringing up the topic to fortuitously highlight the important point that we need to deal with the pedestrian and driverless car interaction problem, and likewise the human driver in another vehicle and driverless car communique problem.

It hasn't become much a "known" or widespread problem as yet, due to the fact that there are so few self-driving cars on our roadways today.

This is undoubtedly going to be a problem in the future and solving it beforehand would seem like a prudent step now.

Conclusion

Those of you that are versed in the self-driving car industry are likely yelling aloud right now that the problem is already solved due to V2P (vehicle-to-pedestrian) electronic communications (or, in the case of cars, V2V or vehicle-to-vehicle electronic messaging).

Yes, it is the case that we are anticipating that driverless cars will electronically communicate with pedestrians via sending messages to their smartphones (or smartwatches, or whatever electronic smarts you might have on you).

That still has to be worked out, plus, you are assuming that pedestrians will have some kind of smart device on them, and that it is able to electronically communicate, and that the communication will occur, and it will happen fast enough, and the pedestrian will pay attention to the smart device when it gets a message, etc.

In brief, putting something directly on the vehicle that is obvious and apparent is the more surefire way of solving the problem (and, it isn't a mutually exclusive deal either since we can certainly implement both at the same time).

One wonders if Baby Yoda would enjoy sitting on the hood of driverless cars and getting a chance to be driven around all day long.

Perhaps we should give it a try?

Do or do not. There is no try.

CHAPTER 3
UGLIEST CARS LOOKS AND AI SELF-DRIVING CARS

CHAPTER 3

UGLIEST CARS LOOKS AND AI SELF-DRIVING CARS

Is your car ugly?

I don't mean whether it possibly has a smattering of unsightly dents or dings, nor whether the paint is chipped and faded.

I'm talking about to the core and down to the bone ugliness.

So ugly that when the car is driven down the street, children get startled and dogs bark incessantly at the vehicle.

So ugly that the car would win hands-down a best (or is it worst?) ugliness contest for cars.

Are you bummed out if your car model is splashed onto headlines as being one of the ugliest cars on the roadways?

Some car owners are enthusiastically proud of the fact that their brand of chosen car is oftentimes listed as one of the ugliest cars ever made.

Perhaps it's an innate contrarian spirit that causes those car owners to intentionally go against the grain of society.

Having an ugly car can be a badge of courage and independence for some. Let the rest of the world groan and whine about the ugliness, while it just reinforces that their chosen brand of car is truthfully a beauteous thing (in the mind of the contrarian).

Honestly, most people tend to scratch their heads when an annual "ugliest car" list is issued for each year's new car models, being puzzled and bewildered as a result of (rightfully, they believe) questioning the veracity of such lists, to begin with.

Some are genuinely skeptical about who gets to make these lists.

Those presumed "authorities" appear to be haughty, and wield their authority high-and-mighty, proclaiming one brand to be ugly and another brand to be alluring and eye-catching, as though a divine spirit has given them great and kingly powers.

Admittedly, some list creators do use surveys to garner public sentiment, along with using sales figures as a surrogate of car-looks impacts, rather than making their own idiosyncratic judgments alone.

If you are curious about which cars have made it onto these glorious lists, here are some examples.

Per Auto Trader has posted this list of the Top 5 ugliest cars ever:

1. Fiat Multipla
2. VW Type 181
3. Nissan Cube
4. Cadillac Seville
5. Sbarro Autobau (concept)
6. Chrysler PT Cruiser

For clarification, I've listed the top six due to the aspect that one of those was a concept car (the Sbarro Autobau), which seems to somewhat inappropriately fit into the realm of real-world on-the-road ugliest cars (you could endlessly rate the zillions of concept cars that have ever been proposed), and so I've opted to include the sixth pole position since it is a car that you could potentially see on the streets.

Speaking of being on the street, some of the cars on the ugliest lists are ones that you've perhaps never had a chance to observe on the highways and byways near you, naturally so, because the number of cars sold for some of these ugliest badged "winners" were not good sellers.

We ought to take a look at other ugliest car lists too, providing a broader perspective on what might have landed on the worst of the worst.

Per Edmunds, here's their list:

1. Lamborghini Veneno
2. Lincoln Versailles
3. Acura ZDX
4. Cadillac Deville
5. Pontiac Aztek
6. Fiat Multipla

Once again, I've listed the top six, though this time I did so to showcase that the Fiat Multipla managed to find its way onto this list and also made it onto the Auto Trader list too (as did the Cadillac Deville), and thus potentially the ugliness is being perceived by more than one authoritative rater at a time.

Some take the aspect of the same cars being on these lists to suggest that those crafting the ugliest cars lists are lemmings and merely fall in line with each other. Of course, one can counter-argue that ugly is ugly, and therefore we'd expect the same or similar set of ugly cars to make these lists.

Another list, not rank-ordered, offers its own set of the ugliest cars and notably one of those on the list might get some of you into a fevered tizzy fit:

- Pontiac Aztek
- Nissan Cube
- Pontiac Trans Sport
- Ford Edsel
- Tesla Cybertruck

Take another look at the list and you'll realize that the newest creation from Elon Musk got onto the list, the Tesla Cybertruck.

For those of you that are Tesla devotees, I'm sure that you immediately recoiled at the inclusion of the recently unveiled Tesla Cybertruck) as having made the list of ugliest looking cars.

On the other hand, returning to the earlier point about being contrarians, there are likely plenty of Tesla lovers that relish the Cybertruck making the ugliest cars list.

They undoubtedly figure might as well let the rest of the Tesla "haters" delude themselves into believing as such (i.e., falsely believing that the Cybertruck is ugly, full-on and unadulterated ugly), meanwhile once the Cybertruck is available for pick-up it will take the world by storm, they so believe.

Is there any science involved in ascertaining which cars are ugly?

Sure, some would assert that the curves of the car, the overall body shape, the streamlined versus tossed together look, these are all hard-and-fast measures to decide whether a vehicle should be classified as ugly or not.

Others eschew this as fake science that is desperately trying to make something tangible and quantitative that is otherwise quite wholly subjective, and purely opinion-based.

Is beauty only in the eye of the beholder?

Equally, is ugliness only in the eye of the beholder?

Some have striven to put an unflinchingly hard-core metric or set of measures together to make this into an unwavering and universally acceptable means of deciding which cars are ugly and even how much ugliness they imbue.

Balderdash, others say, and point out that it all depends upon your cultural immersion and societal predisposition as to what constitutes ugly versus not ugly.

Here's an interesting question to ponder: *Will AI-based true self-driving cars eventually make their way onto the ugliest car lists, and if so, does it matter?*

Bet you hadn't thought about that.

We'll gradually see the emergence of true self-driving cars onto our streets and freeways, driving among us, and become prevalent as an everyday mode of transport.

When that happens, are they susceptible to getting ranked as an ugly car?

Will it make a difference if they do get onto such a "vaunted" list?

Let's unpack the matter and see.

The Levels Of Self-Driving Cars

It is important to clarify what I mean when referring to AI-based true self-driving cars.

True self-driving cars are ones that the AI drives the car entirely on its own and there isn't any human assistance during the driving task.

These driverless vehicles are considered a Level 4 and Level 5, while a car that requires a human driver to co-share the driving effort is usually considered at a Level 2 or Level 3. The cars that co-share the driving task are described as being semi-autonomous, and typically contain a variety of automated add-on's that are referred to as ADAS (Advanced Driver-Assistance Systems).

There is not yet a true self-driving car at Level 5, which we don't yet even know if this will be possible to achieve, and nor how long it will take to get there.

Meanwhile, the Level 4 efforts are gradually trying to get some traction by undergoing very narrow and selective public roadway trials, though there is controversy over whether this testing should be allowed per se (we are all life-or-death guinea pigs in an experiment taking place on our highways and byways, some point out).

Since semi-autonomous cars require a human driver, the adoption of those types of cars won't be markedly different than driving conventional vehicles, so there's not much new per se to cover about them on this topic (though, as you'll see in a moment, the points next made are generally applicable).

For semi-autonomous cars, it is important that the public be forewarned about a disturbing aspect that's been arising lately, namely that in spite of those human drivers that keep posting videos of themselves falling asleep at the wheel of a Level 2 or Level 3 car, we all need to avoid being misled into believing that the driver can take away their attention from the driving task while driving a semi-autonomous car.

You are the responsible party for the driving actions of the vehicle, regardless of how much automation might be tossed into a Level 2 or Level 3.

Self-Driving Cars And Ugly Lists

For Level 4 and Level 5 true self-driving vehicles, there won't be a human driver involved in the driving task.

All occupants will be passengers.

The AI is doing the driving.

Pundits suggest that by-and-large the use of driverless cars will be for ride-sharing purposes (see my analysis of this point, **here**).

It is assumed that a new era of mobility will arise, allowing a mobility-for-all advent. Those today that are mobility hampered or disadvantaged will finally be able to readily and inexpensively have access to car transportation.

A boon for society.

If that's going to be the case, ask yourself a pointed question.

Do you care what a ride-sharing car that is giving you a lift looks like?

In other words, a ride-sharing car, regardless of human-driven or AI-driven, comes to pick you up, and once it arrives, most would say that the looks of the vehicle make no difference as to whether or not you are willing to take the ride.

All you care about is that the car is operable, in good enough condition to reliably provide transport, and will safely make its way to your destination.

Have you ever decided to not get into a ride-sharing car simply based on whether it is blue or red or orange in color, or maybe due to the overall shape of the car?

Unlikely.

To be clear, if the car looks to be in bad condition and has been through the wringer, I think we'd all be suspect about how the driver is taking care of the vehicle, and rightfully avoid taking the car on any ride-sharing journey unless absolutely desperate for a ride.

On looks alone, if a particular brand of car is considered by list-makers as looking ugly, would that change your willingness to go for a ride when requesting a rise-sharing lift?

Most probably not.

The point being that if driverless cars are not going to be owned by individuals (which, I claim is a misleading and somewhat false assertion, see my analysis **at this link**), and exist in fleets of ride-sharing vehicles, the looks of the car are no longer pertinent.

Presumably, the reason that ugliness makes a difference today is due to whether consumers buying cars want to have the stigma or not of owning and driving around in a so-called ugly car.

Take away the consumer ownership part of the equation, and ugliness falls by the wayside.

Period, end of story.

Maybe.

Why wouldn't it fall by the wayside?

One theory is that people are going to intrinsically feel good or bad about themselves as a result of the looks of a car that they are riding in, even despite not owning the car per se.

Place yourself into the future, when there are nearly only and all driverless cars, while conventional human-driven cars are as scarce as hen's teeth.

You are going to go on a first date and want to impress the other person.

Using your smartphone, you request a ride-sharing vehicle to come and get you and will have it to take you to your date's place, and then the driverless car will take you two to the movies.

Do you care about the looks of the self-driving car?

It seems quite possible.

You want to impress your date, so you avoid taking one of those "ugly" cars and instead make sure to request a car that is known for being beauteous.

Here's another reason that looks might make a difference.

If you agree that self-driving cars will be predominantly a part of large fleets, the odds are that the fleet owner would want to get pretty much the same brand and model for their fleet, leveraging sensibly any potential economies of scale (the fleet owner could more readily perform maintenance and care on one selected brand or model, versus dealing with a multitude of brands and models).

I've previously pointed out that we are possibly heading toward a world wherein you can't tell one self-driving car from another (see **the link here**).

What I mean is that if fleets have thousands upon thousands of the same brand and model of a driverless car, you'll see that particular brand and model all the time, and not be able to readily discern one driverless from another.

When a driverless car comes to pick you up, there is likely to be a lot less variety of models and brands of cars, thus, you'll statistically see the same brand or model each time.

Eventually, this might pressure fleet owners to differentiate themselves from other driverless car fleets, and thus they might opt to buy their next brand and model based on how the car looks. Thus, once again, the notion of being an ugly car comes back around and might be a strategic differentiator for why people choose a particular driverless car fleet ride-sharing service (wherein people believe that driverless cars X are less or more alluring to ride in than driverless cars Y, simply by looks alone).

Now, keep in mind, the aforementioned refers to a somewhat far away future.

For now, it is going to take years upon years for self-driving cars to come into the marketplace, likely many decades.

Shifting then our attention to contemporary times, let's further consider the ugliness factor.

Today's Self-Driving Cars And Ugliness

Self-driving cars tend to have a rooftop rack of sensors, including cameras, radar, LIDAR, and other such sensory devices.

You've most certainly have seen videos or pictures of driverless cars, or perhaps encountered ones that have happened to be on the roadways near you.

In the earlier days of driverless car dreams, the thought was that a self-driving car would be a new kind of car, being completely redesigned from the ground up. Though this is indeed taking place, and many are stridently heading in that direction, the more expedient method to getting up-to-speed involves taking a conventional car and retrofitting it to have driverless tech.

When you see a conventional car that has been augmented with self-driving tech, what do you think about it?

Does the rooftop of all those gadgets and gizmos make the car look ugly?

The odds are that there are also additional gadgets and gizmos mounted on the sides and both ends of the vehicle.

I suppose that some people might think they've just seen a Frankenstein car going down the street.

Driverless cars might today be perceived as having a bunch of electronics jammed onto them, appearing to be a jumble of rotating this and hanging out that.

Ugly!

Ugly?

I'd bet that most people are fascinated to see such a car and aren't immediately leaping to a judgment that the driverless car looks ugly.

It looks like, well, the future.

The newness factor tends to downplay the looks and instead grab our interest out of curiosity and amazement.

Okay, once those driverless cars are in droves, and we see them each and every day, and we drive near to them in traffic, and we get used to them as being "fellow" drivers, it could be that we no longer view those cars as extraordinary.

In that case, maybe the looks come back into play again.

Conclusion

Speaking of being a contrarian, it's my position that we aren't going to have only a handful of fleet owners that command all self-driving cars.

Individual ownership of self-driving cars is still a possibility, and I argue that it is likely, partially due to the aspect that each of us will have an opportunity to make money from owning a driverless car. Right now, we own cars that sit and do nothing for 95% of the time, a costly asset that is woefully underutilized.

By owning a self-driving car, you could use it to get to work, and then the rest of the workday it is providing ride-sharing, bringing in the bucks for you, making it into a money-making asset rather than today's (essentially) money-losing asset.

Would looks matter when we still have individual ownership of cars, in this case, self-driving cars?

Humans seem to care about looks, which crops up in most things that we do or own.

The idea that we'll dispense with rating the looks of anything, including self-driving cars, would seemingly go against the very nature of human behavior.

We are all preprogrammed to judge a book by its cover, and no matter how hard we try to suppress that innate urge, it inevitably and inextricably re-emerges.

Time will tell, and that's the ugly truth on the matter.

.

CHAPTER 4

MACGYVER SHREWDNESS AND AI SELF-DRIVING CARS

CHAPTER 4
MACGYVER SHREWDNESS AND AI SELF-DRIVING CARS

MacGyver solved it again!

Who or what is a MacGyver, you might wonder?

Well, most people have heard of MacGyver, the TV series and main character that manages to always find a clever means to extricate himself from some puzzling predicament, using his wits to devise a solution out of rather everyday items.

Fans know that he carries a Swiss Army knife, rather than a gun, since he believes that using his creativity and inventiveness will always allow him to deal with any untoward circumstance (the knife is handy when you need to defuse a bomb, or when you need to take apart a toaster and reuse its electronics for a completely different purpose and ultimately save your life accordingly).

Turns out that you don't necessarily need to have ever seen the show or watched any YouTube clips and yet still nonetheless might know what it signifies to be a "MacGyver" in dealing with a thorny task (it has become part of our lexicon of speaking).

In short, we now consider any kind of innovative solution to be characterized as a MacGyver-like approach, assuming that it is an elegant and somewhat simple solution to a seemingly intractable problem.

Let's parse that statement.

One crucial element is that the problem itself has to be somewhat bedeviling.

If the problem is straightforward and not filled with complications, you presumably could solve it with just your ordinary noggin and not need to put on a MacGyver-like thinking cap.

Another vital aspect is that the solution cannot be blatantly obvious.

In other words, if a monkey could immediately see how to solve the problem, you don't need to rachet up into the stratosphere of problem-solving and instead can just do a grab-and-go to solve the matter at hand.

Okay, so the problem needs to be tough or relatively intractable, and the solution has to be non-obvious and requires a stretch of the imagination to come up with.

What else?

The problem needs to be solvable.

This is important and often not readily knowable at the start of the problem-solving process.

Oftentimes, when a problem is presented to you or emerges, you aren't exactly sure whether there are any means to solve it.

As such, you might explore a variety of potential solutions, and in so doing discover a whole bunch of potential solutions that aren't viable to solve the actual problem.

In the case of the MacGyver lore, he always does find a solution, which is heartwarming, but you can't expect in real life that a solution is always findable.

We can say that it is helpful perhaps to assume that a solution is findable, which can boost your spirits when in the throes of trying to solve a hairy problem and might inspire you.

For those that sometimes give up right away and assume there is no solution, it is as though they have tossed in the towel and aren't, therefore, going to put in the energy to try and ferret out a solution.

That being said, there is also the real-world aspect that ultimately there might not be a solution (unlike the TV show, which always provides a fairy book happy ending).

An added twist is that maybe there is a solution, yet only time will allow the solution to be realized, and thus you might not immediately be able to solve the predicament, even though you've divined how it could be solved.

How could you have discovered a solution and yet there is a lapse in time before you can solve the problem?

An easy example would be a candle that once lit will slowly burn through a rope, and once the rope is cut by the fire, it then releases you from a trap.

In that example, you knew a viable solution, yet it took a while for the solution to be carried out.

Suppose though that you had no evident means of lighting the candle?

This becomes another form of problem, one that is connected to the larger problem of presumably being trapped. It is a "new" problem in that it ties to your solution and might or might not directly be considered part of the originating problem of having been trapped.

Perhaps there's a box of matches in the other room, which if you could reach it, you'd grab a match to light the candle to then burn through the rope to release you from the trap (reminiscent of a Rube Goldberg arrangement).

Your proposed solution is now stopped in the quest of getting those matches.

Time might unwind and it turns out that the box of matches gets knocked off a table due to a wind gust that comes up, spilling the matches, one of which rolls to into your trapped area.

Anyway, the point being that it is not necessarily the case that you will always be able to perform a MacGyver instantaneously and must allow for time to go forward for a solution to become viable or to emerge (for a TV show, they need to wrap-up the solution on a timely basis since the show only has thirty minutes or an hour, while in real life things might be of much longer duration).

To be a true MacGyver-like scenario, we usually expect that whatever solution is devised will be straightforward *and* elegant at the same time.

This elegance criteria can be hard to boil down and explain in words. It is one of those things whereby if you see it, you'll be able to decide whether it was elegant or not (akin to beauty being in the eye of the beholder).

We'll try an extreme case to illustrate by most standards something that would not be considered elegant.

This is going to be somewhat gruesome, so ready yourself.

Suppose that a solution involved having to cut off an arm to save yourself (as depicted in the movie *127 Hours* about the real-world case of outdoorsman Aron Ralston).

Yikes!

Yes, it did solve the problem, due to being stuck or wedged into a canyon slot and the prospect of dying there was looming over Aron, though the act of rendering the solution was certainly stomach-churning to watch even when fictionally portrayed, and quite incredible to think that someone could perform the act.

He seemingly had tried to find any and all other possible solutions, yet none of them worked or were feasible to carry out.

This was a last resort solution.

Was it elegant in the sense of what we mean when saying that a MacGyver solution is generally supposed to exhibit some form of elegance or grace, as it were?

Hard to say.

Somehow, it doesn't smack of elegance, though admittedly he did live to tell the tale.

Part of the reason that I picked that example was to highlight that sometimes we are faced with a problem that involves life-or-death.

Sure, in the TV show, MacGyver is nearly always faced with a life-or-death predicament, but for most real-world applications of the MacGyver-like approach, you usually aren't dealing with life-or-death matters.

The point being that sometimes the MacGyver is handy for ordinary matters involving difficult problems, while in other instances the whole enchilada might be on the line.

This brings us to an important consideration about how we think as humans, along with how AI systems are being crafted and the limits of what they to-date have been able to achieve.

Please be aware that the AI of today is not even close to being anything equivalent to true human intelligence, which might be a shocking point for some to realize, but nonetheless is indeed the case.

Sure, there are pockets of situations whereby an AI application has seemingly been able to perform a task as well as a human might, these are constantly in the news.

That though is a far cry from being able to exhibit a full range of intelligence and pass any kind of Turing Test.

Today's AI systems tend to be classified as having narrow AI, meaning that they can possibly "solve" a narrow problem, meanwhile such an AI system is not AGI (Artificial General Intelligence) and lacks human qualities such as common-sense reasoning.

In fact, one significant concern about the rampant use of Machine Learning (ML) and Deep Learning (DL) is that those computationally based patterns matching algorithms tend to be brittle, susceptible to falling out-of-step when faced with exceptions or unusual cases.

The odds are that any situation requiring or deploying a MacGyver is by definition bound to be an exceptional or unusual case (otherwise, you'd use some other brute force or ordinary solving methods).

Here's an intriguing question to ponder: *"Will the advent of AI-based true self-driving cars potentially be stymied by exceptional or unusual circumstances, and if so, could the use of MacGyver-like approaches help overcome those impediments?"*

The answer is that yes, so-called edge cases (another term for an exception or unusual instances) are a significant concern about the safety of true self-driving cars, and yes, if AI systems could employ MacGyver-like capabilities it might help to deal with those tough moments.

Let's unpack the matter and see.

The Levels Of Self-Driving Cars

It is important to clarify what I mean when referring to AI-based true self-driving cars.

True self-driving cars are ones that the AI drives the car entirely on its own and there isn't any human assistance during the driving task.

These driverless vehicles are considered a Level 4 and Level 5, while a car that requires a human driver to co-share the driving effort is usually considered at a Level 2 or Level 3. The cars that co-share the driving task are described as being semi-autonomous, and typically contain a variety of automated add-on's that are referred to as ADAS (Advanced Driver-Assistance Systems).

There is not yet a true self-driving car at Level 5, which we don't yet even know if this will be possible to achieve, and nor how long it will take to get there.

Meanwhile, the Level 4 efforts are gradually trying to get some traction by undergoing very narrow and selective public roadway trials, though there is controversy over whether this testing should be allowed per se (we are all life-or-death guinea pigs in an experiment taking place on our highways and byways, some point out).

Since semi-autonomous cars require a human driver, the adoption of those types of cars won't be markedly different than driving conventional vehicles, so there's not much new per se to cover about them on this topic (though, as you'll see in a moment, the points next made are generally applicable).

For semi-autonomous cars, it is important that the public be forewarned about a disturbing aspect that's been arising lately, namely that in spite of those human drivers that keep posting videos of themselves falling asleep at the wheel of a Level 2 or Level 3 car, we all need to avoid being misled into believing that the driver can take away their attention from the driving task while driving a semi-autonomous car.

You are the responsible party for the driving actions of the vehicle, regardless of how much automation might be tossed into a Level 2 or Level 3.

Self-Driving Cars And MacGyver

For Level 4 and Level 5 true self-driving vehicles, there won't be a human driver involved in the driving task.

All occupants will be passengers.

The AI is doing the driving.

To date, the efforts to devise self-driving cars have generally consisted of getting the AI to be able to drive in relatively ordinary driving situations.

This makes sense, namely, get the "easier" stuff done first (for clarity, none of this is especially easy), involving having the AI driving system be able to drive in a somewhat calm neighborhood or a relatively everyday freeway traffic setting.

Furthermore, if you are using collected driving data to train an ML/DL system, the odds are that most of the driving data is also primarily about day-to-day driving and bereft of those out-of-the-ordinary driving occasions.

Think about your own driving efforts.

Much of the time, you are driving along, mulling over what you'll eat for dinner that night or replaying in your mind that difficult conversation you had with your boss the other day, and not seemingly paying rapt attention to the roadway.

On and on this "mindless" driving often occurs.

Then, there are those rarer moments (hopefully rare), when something extraordinary yanks you out of your complacency and you need to immediately respond.

That's when the shucks hit the fan, if you know what I mean.

It could be a life-or-death circumstance involving having to size-up in real-time a difficult problem facing you in the traffic setting, and of which you need to assess what your options might be, including having to enact those options soon enough and sufficiently to avoid death or destruction.

All in a whisper of a moment.

Most would concede that today's AI driving systems are decidedly not yet ready to cope with those moments if the problem isn't one that the AI driving system hasn't already "seen" previously or been otherwise pre-programmed to handle.

A novel or surprise situation is not good for AI driving systems, right now, and thus not good for human passengers, nor pedestrians, nor other nearby human-driven cars.

What to do about those edge problems?

The usual answer is to keep pushing along on roadway trials and collecting lots of driving data, and hopefully, eventually, all possible permutations and possibilities of driving situations will have been captured, and then presumably analyzed so they can be dealt with.

One has to be dubious about such an approach.

A leading self-driving car company is Waymo, which has accumulated around 20+ million roadway miles all told, and though it seems at first glance an impressive number, keep in mind that humans drive over 3 trillion miles, per year, and so the odds of finding a needle in a haystack of a lot lesser miles is probabilistically less likely.

Insiders of the self-driving car industry also know that miles are not just miles, no matter which self-driving car company is doing roadway tryouts, meaning that if you drive in the same places over-and-over, those miles are not necessarily as revealing as driving in a more radically changing and variety of roadways and road conditions.

Another offered approach involves doing simulations.

Automakers and self-driving tech firms do tend to use simulations, in addition to driving on roadways, though there is an ongoing debate about whether simulations should be undertaken prior to allowing public roadway use, or whether it is satisfactory to do both at the same time, plus there is debate too about whether simulations are adequate as a substitute for driven miles (once again, it depends upon the type of simulation undertaken and how it is constructed and utilized).

Some believe that AI driving systems ought to have a MacGyver-like component, prepared to tackle those extraordinary problems that arise while driving.

It would not especially be based on prior oddball or edge case situations, and instead, be a generalized component that could be invoked when the rest of the AI driving system has been unable to resolve a playing out circumstance.

In some manner of speaking, it would be like AGI but specifically in the domain of driving cars.
Is that even possible?

Some argue that AGI is either AGI or it is not, thus, trying to suggest that you might construct an AGI for a specific domain is counter to the AGI notion overall.

Others argue that when seated in a car, a human driver is making use of AGI in the domain of driving a car, not solving world hunger or having to deal with just any problems, and thus we ought to be able to focus attention to an AGI for the driving domain alone.

Hey, maybe we should apply MacGyver to the problem of solving edge cases and find an elegant solution to doing so, which might or might not consist of employing a MacGyver into the AI of the driving system.

That's a mind twister, for sure.

Conclusion

A handy paper on the AI challenges in dealing with MacGyver-like problems was written by researchers Sarahthy and Scheutz at Tufts University. The authors point out that an AI system would likely need to be able to undertake numerous arduous tasks and sub-tasks in performing any MacGyver-like situation, including being able to do impasse detection, domain transformation, problem restructuring, experimentation, discovery detection, domain extension, and so on.

Essentially, it is a very hard problem to get an AI system to act like MacGyver, regardless of whether there is a Swiss Army knife available or not.

In the case of an AI driving system, realize too that the MacGyver component would need to act in real-time, having only split seconds to ascertain what action to take.

Plus, the actions taken are most likely linked to life-or-death consequences, including too the qualms associated with the Trolley problem (this involves having to make choices between which deaths or injuries to incur versus other sets of deaths or injuries, see my explanation at **the link here**).

If you say that we ought not to seek a MacGyver-like capability, it raises the obvious question as to what alternatives do we have, and meanwhile, self-driving cars are proceeding along, absent such an ingenious or even similar capacity.

There is also the belief that if we could do MacGyver for the AI driving domain, we might be able to start stretching it to other domains, allowing a stepwise achievement of an AGI across all domains, though that's a quite argumentative contention and a story for another day.

MacGyver is known for saying that you can do anything you wanna do if you put your mind to it.

Can we get AI to do anything we want it to do if we put our minds to it?

Time will tell.

.

CHAPTER 5
STRONG VS WEAK AI AND AI SELF-DRIVING CARS

CHAPTER 5
STRONG VS WEAK AI AND AI SELF-DRIVING CARS

Strong AI.

Weak AI.

Strong versus weak AI.

Or, if you prefer, you can state it as weak versus strong AI (it's Okay to be listed in either order, yet still has the same spice, as it were).

If you've read much about AI in the popular press, the odds are that you've seen references to so-called strong AI and so-called weak AI, and yet the odds further are that both of those phrases have been used wrongly and offer misleading and confounding impressions.

Time to set the record straight.

First, let's consider what is being incorrectly stated.

Some speak of weak AI as though it is AI that is wimpy and not up to the same capabilities as strong AI, including that weak AI is decidedly slower, or much less optimized, or otherwise inevitably and unarguably feebler in its AI capacities.

No, that's not it.

Another form of distortion is to ascribe that "narrow" AI, which generally refers to AI that will only work in a narrowly defined domain such as in a specific say medical use or in a particular financial analysis use, can be ascribed as being the same as weak AI, while presumably strong AI is broader and more all-encompassing.

No, that's not it either.

And, so on, the mistaken uses go.

One might be sympathetic and acknowledge that the words "weak" and "strong" have everyday connotations that would lead you to assume that those forms of interpretation in an AI context might be seemingly correct.

Unfortunately, that's not the actual case.

Being frank, this is just not what weak AI and strong AI were originally coined to mean.

Those versed in the AI field are likely to lament that the words "weak" and "strong" were originally anointed as labels at all, since doing so has generated a sordid trail and a life of its own about what people assume or think those words mean in an AI context.

Over time, many have either failed to study properly and learn what weak AI and strong AI were meant to describe (twisted and distorted by those culprits that are lazy or ill-informed about the use of the lexicon), or some have opted to hijack the phrasing for other innumerable uses (doing so willfully, adding fuel to the misinterpretation fire).

I'm not saying that you cannot choose to re-purpose and re-flavor terminology, only that doing so creates added confusion and causes discussions to become burdened unnecessarily with tangents over what one person means in comparison to what someone else means.

In essence, yes, a rose is a rose by any other name, but an apple is not an orange, even if you decide to one day shift toward calling oranges by the word apples.

Now that I've covered what those AI vocab monikers don't mean, let's get to brass tacks and see what they do mean (or, at least what the original meaning consisted of).

Meaning Of Strong AI And Weak AI

Hark back to an earlier era of AI, around the late 1970s and early 1980s, a period of time that was characterized as the first era of AI flourishment, which you might know as a time when Knowledge-Based Systems (KBS) and Expert Systems (ES) were popular.

The latest era, today, which some consider the second era of AI flourishment, seems to have become known as the time of Machine Learning (ML) and Deep Learning (DL).

Using a season oriented metaphor, the current era is depicted as the AI Spring, while the period between the first era and this now existent second era has been called the AI Winter (doing so to suggest that things were either dormant or slowed-down like how a winter season can clamp down via snow and other dampening weatherly conditions).

The first era consisted of quite a bit of handwringing about whether AI was going to become sentient and if so, how would we get there.

Even during this second era, there are still similar discussions and debates taking place now, though the first era really seemed to fully take the matter in-hand and many slews of philosophers joined onto the AI bandwagon as to what the future might hold and how AI could be or might not become truly intelligent.

Into that fray came the birth of the monikers of weak AI and strong AI.

Most would agree that the verbiage originated in a paper by philosopher John Searle entitled "Minds, Brains, And Programs," though this is not quite the remembrance of everyone at the time in the sense that some suggest the wording of "weak" and "strong" was already floating around, meanwhile, Searle's paper put it firmly into writing and became a handy and tangible flashpoint on the matter (and, for that, he certainly deserves due credit).

What was the weak AI and what was the strong AI?

They are philosophical differences about how AI might ultimately be achieved, assuming that you agree as to what it means to achieve AI (more on this in a moment).

Let's see what Searle said about defining the terminology of weak AI:

"According to weak AI, the principal value of the computer in the study of the mind is that it gives us a very powerful tool. For example, it enables us to formulate and test hypotheses in a more rigorous and precise fashion."

And, furthermore, he indicated this about strong AI:

"But according to strong AI, the computer is not merely a tool in the study of the mind; rather, the appropriately programmed computer really is a mind, in the sense that computers given the right programs can be literally said to understand and have other cognitive states."

With this added clarification:

"In strong AI, because the programmed computer has cognitive states, the programs are not mere tools that enable us to test psychological explanations; rather, the programs are themselves the explanations."

The rest of his famous (now infamous) paper then proceeds to indicate that he has "no objection to the claims of weak AI," and thus he doesn't tackle particularly the weak AI side of things, and instead his focus goes mainly toward the portent of strong AI.

In short, he doesn't have much faith or belief that strong AI is anything worth writing home about either, he says this:

"On the argument advanced here only a machine could think, and only very special kinds of machines, namely brains and machines with internal causal powers equivalent to those of brains. And that is why strong AI has little to tell us about thinking, since it is not about machines but about programs, and no program by itself is sufficient for thinking."

Here's what that signifies, at least as has been interpreted by some.

Conventional AI is presumably doomed in trying to reach true AI if you stick with using "computer programs" since those programs aren't ever going to cut it, and lack the needed capabilities to embody those things we associate with thinking and sentience. Humans and animals have a kind of intentionality, somehow arising from the use of our brains, and for those that believe true AI requires that intentionality, you are barking up the wrong tree via the pursuit of "computer programs" (they are the wrong stuff and can't go that high up the intelligence ladder).

All of this presupposes two key assumptions or propositions that Seale lays out:

1. "Intentionality in human beings (and animals) is a product of causal features of the brain…"
2. "Instantiating a computer program is never by itself a sufficient condition of intentionality."

If you goal then is to devise a computer program that can think, you are on a fool's errand and won't ever get there, though, it isn't completely foolish because you might well learn a lot along the way and could have some really cool results and insights, but it isn't going to be a thinker.

I believe it is self-evident that this is a deeply intriguing philosophical consideration, one worthy of scholars and others pontificating about.

Does this make a difference for everyday AI work that those making AI-based systems such as Alexa or Siri or robots that function on a manufacturing line are going to be worrying about and losing sleep over?

No.

To clarify, we are a long, long, long, long way from crafting AI systems that are able to exhibit human-level intelligence in any genuine meaning of the range, scope, and depth of human intelligence.

That's a shocker to some that keep hearing about AI systems that are as adept as humans.

Take a slow and measured breath and keep reading herein.

Achieving True AI Is The Hearty Question

I had earlier mentioned narrow AI.

There are some AI applications that do seemingly well in narrow domains, though maybe they should have a Surgeon General type small print that identifies the numerous caveats and limitations about what that AI can really do.

AI systems today cannot undertake or showcase common-sense reasoning, which I believe we all agree that humans generally have (for those snickering about humans having or not having common-sense reasoning, yes, there are people that we know that seems to at times lack common-sense, but that's not the same as what overall is considered common-sense reasoning and don't conflate those two into meaninglessness).

To insiders of AI, today's AI applications are narrow AI, and not yet AGI (Artificial General Intelligence) systems, which is yet another term that is being used to get around the fact that "AI" has been watered down as terminology and used for anything that people want to say is AI, meanwhile there are others striving mightily to get to the purists' version of AI, which would be AGI.

The debate about weak AI and strong AI is aimed at those that wonder whether we will be able to someday achieve true AI.

True AI is a loaded term that needs some clarification.

One version of true AI is an AI system that can pass the Turing Test, a simple yet telling kind of test that involves asking an AI system questions and asking a human being questions, essentially two distinct players in a game of wielding intelligence, of sorts, and if you cannot tell which is which, presumably the AI is the "equivalent" of human intelligence since it was indistinguishable from a human exhibiting intelligence.

Though the Turing Test is handy, and a frequently invoked tool for judging AI's efforts to become true AI, it does have its own downsides and problematic considerations.

Anyway, how can we craft AI to succeed at the Turing Test and have AI be ostensibly indistinguishable from human intelligence?

One belief is that we'll need to embody into the AI system the same kind of intentionality, casualty, thinking, and essence of sentience that exists in humans (and to some extent, in animals).

As a side note, the day that we reach AI sentience is often referred to as the singularity, and some believe that it will inevitably be reached and we'll have then the equivalent of human intelligence, whilst others believe that the AI will exceed human intelligence and we will actually arrive at a form of AI super-intelligence.

Keep in mind that not everyone agrees with the precondition of needing to discover and re-invent artificial intentionality, asserting that we can nonetheless arrive at AI that exhibits human intelligence yet do so without tossing into the cart this squishy stuff referred to as intentionality and its vagrants.

Anyway, setting aside that last aspect, the other big question is whether "computer programs" will be the appropriate tool to get us there (whatever the *there* might be).

This brings up another definitional consideration.

What do you mean by computer programs?

At the time when this debate first flourished, computer programs generally meant hand-crafted coding using both conventional and somewhat unconventional programming languages, exemplified by programs such as ELIZA by Weizenbaum and SHRDLU by Winograd.

Today, we are using Machine Learning and Deep Learning, so the obvious question on the minds of those that are still mulling over weak AI and strong AI would be whether the use of ML/DL constitutes "computer programs" or not.

Have we progressed past the old-time computer programs and advanced into whatever ML/DL is, such that we are no longer seemingly have this albatross around our neck that computer programs aren't the rocket ship that can get us to this desired moon?

Well, that opens another can of worms, though it is pretty much the case that most would agree that ML/DL is still a "computer program" in the meaning of even the 1980s expression, so, if you buy into the argument that any use of or a variant of computer programs is insufficient to arrive at thinking AI, we are still in the doom-and-gloom state of affairs.

Searle though does cover the ML/DL topic to some degree since he mentions that a man-made machine could think if it:

"Assuming it is possible to produce artificially a machine with a nervous system, neurons with axons and dendrites, and all the rest of it, sufficiently like ours, again the answer to the question seems to be obvious, yes. If you can exactly duplicate the causes, you could duplicate the effects. And indeed it might be possible to produce consciousness, intentionality, and all the rest of it using some other sorts of chemical principles than those that human beings use."

Please be aware that today's ML/DL is a far cry from being the same as human neurons and a human brain.

At best, it is a crude and extremely simplified simulation, usually deploying Artificial Neural Networks (ANNs), way below anything approaching a human biological equivalent. We might someday get closer and indeed some believe we will achieve the equivalent, but don't be holding your breath for the now.

Bringing us home to the argument about weak and strong AI, no matter what you do in either the case of weak AI or strong AI, here's where you'll land as per Searle:

"But could something think, understand, and so on solely in virtue of being a computer with the right sort of program? Could instantiating a program, the right program of course, by itself be a sufficient condition of understanding?"

And his clear-cut answer is: "This I think is the right question to ask, though it is usually confused with one or more of the earlier questions, and the answer to it is no."

Ouch!

That smarts.

There is nonetheless a glimmer of hope for strong AI, as it could apparently be potentially turned into something that could achieve the thinking brand of AI (says Searle): "Any attempt literally to create intentionality artificially (strong AI) could not succeed just by designing programs but would have to duplicate the causal powers of the human brain."

Practical Significance For Today

I hope it is obvious that the original meaning associated with weak and strong AI is far afield of what the popular press tends to use those catchy phrases for today.

As mentioned, some use weak AI to refer to narrow AI, but that's not the spirit nor significance of what weak AI means in its original context.

Some use weak AI to suggest an AI system is feeble, but that's also not at all what the original meaning of weak AI is about.

When trying to point out to people that their use of weak AI and strong AI is not aligned with the original meanings, they usually get huffy and tell you to not be such a stickler.

Or, they tell you to knock the cobwebs out of your mind and become hipper with the present age.

Fine, I suppose, you can change up the meaning if you want, just please be aware that it is not the same as the original.

This comes up in numerous applied uses of AI.

For example, consider the emergence of AI-based true self-driving cars.

True self-driving cars are ones that the AI drives the car entirely on its own and there isn't any human assistance during the driving task.

These driverless vehicles are considered a Level 4 and Level 5, while a car that requires a human driver to co-share the driving effort is usually considered at a Level 2 or Level 3. The cars that co-share the driving task are described as being semi-autonomous, and typically contain a variety of automated add-on's that are referred to as ADAS (Advanced Driver-Assistance Systems).

There is not yet a true self-driving car at Level 5, which we don't yet even know if this will be possible to achieve, and nor how long it will take to get there.

Meanwhile, the Level 4 efforts are gradually trying to get some traction by undergoing very narrow and selective public roadway trials, though there is controversy over whether this testing should be allowed per se (we are all life-or-death guinea pigs in an experiment taking place on our highways and byways, some point out).

Some of the media describe the semi-autonomous ADAS as weak AI, while the autonomous AI to be strong AI.

Well, that's not aligned with the original definitions of weak AI and strong AI.

You have to be willing to put to the side the original definitions if you are seeking to use those terms in that manner.

Personally, I don't like it.

Similarly, I don't like it when the weak AI and strong AI are used to characterize the difference between autonomous AI.

For example, some say that Level 4 is weak AI, while Level 5 is strong AI, but this once again is nonsensical in the nature of what those terms were intended to signify.

If you genuinely want to try and apply the argument to true self-driving cars, there is an ongoing dispute as to whether driverless cars will need to exhibit "intentionality" to be sufficiently safe for our public roadways.

In other words, can we craft AI without any seeming embodiment of intentionality and yet nonetheless have that AI be good enough to trust AI-based self-driving cars cruising around on our highways, byways, and everyday streets?

It's a complex debate, and no one yet knows whether the driving domain can be considered limited enough in scope that such intentionality is not a necessity, plus, the question within a question is what might be rated as safe or safe enough for society to accept self-driving cars as fellow drivers.

Conclusion

For those of you wanting to get further into the weeds on this topic, you'll also want to get introduced to the Chinese Room Argument (CRA), a foil used in Searle's argument and something that has become a storied punching bag in the halls of AI and philosophy.

That's a story for another day.

Practitioners of AI might see this whole discussion about weak AI and strong AI as academic and much ado about nothing.

Use those phrases whatever way you want, some say.

Hold your horses.

Perhaps we ought to heed the words of William Shakespeare: "Words without thoughts never to heaven go."

The words we use do matter, and especially in the high stakes aims and outcomes of AI.

CHAPTER 6

TROLLEY PROBLEM AND AI SELF-DRIVING CARS

CHAPTER 6
TROLLEY PROBLEM
AND
AI SELF-DRIVING CARS

One of the most controversial topics for insiders that know about AI-based true self-driving cars is the famous (or infamous) Trolley Problem.

Let's unpack the matter and see what we can reveal.

Be aware that this discussion will be a bit longer in length than the normal coverage of such topics in my column, but it seems worthwhile in order to hopefully serve as a wake-up call on an altogether contentious topic that has indubitably suffered from confusion, unsupported denials, catcalls intended to demean the matter, and otherwise seemingly been dismissed out-of-hand.

I'd like to see if we can give the matter its serious consideration and due.

The place to start entails clarifying what the Trolley Problem consists of.

Turns out that it is an ethically stimulating thought experiment that traces back to the early 1900s. As such, the topic has been around for quite a while and more recently has become generally associated with the advent of self-driving cars.

In short, imagine that a trolley is going down the tracks and there is a fork up ahead. If the trolley continues in its present course, alas there is someone stuck on the tracks further along and they will get run down and killed.

You are standing next to a switch that will allow you to redirect the trolley into the forking rail track and thus avoid killing the person.

Presumably, obviously, you would invoke the switchover.

But there is a hideous twist, namely that the forked track also has someone entangled on it, and by diverting the trolley you will kill that person instead.

This is one of those no-win situations.

Whichever choice you make, a person is going to be killed.

You might be tempted to say that you do not have to make a choice and therefore you can readily sidestep the whole matter.

Not really, since by doing nothing you are essentially "agreeing" to have the person killed that is on the straight-ahead path. You cannot seemingly avoid your culpability by shrugging your shoulders and opting to do nothing, instead, you are inextricably intertwined into the situation.

Given this preliminary setup of the Trolley Problem as a lose-lose with one person at stake in your choice of either option, it does not especially spark an ethical dilemma since each outcome is woefully considered the same.

The matter is usually altered in various ways to try and see how you might respond to a more ethically challenging circumstance.

For example, suppose you are able to discern that the straight-ahead track has a child on it, while the forked track has an adult.

What now?

Well, you might attempt to justify using the switch to get the trolley to fork onto the track with the adult, doing so under the logic that the adult has already lived some substantive part of their life, while the child is only at the beginning of their life and perhaps ought to be given a chance for a longer existence.

How does that seem to you?

Some buy into it, some do not.

There are those that might argue that every person has an equal "value" of living and it is untoward to prejudge that the child should live while the adult is to die.

Some would argue that the adult should be the one that is kept alive since they have already shown that they can survive longer than the child.

Here's another variation.

Both are adults, and the one on the forked path is Einstein.

Does this change your viewpoint about which way to direct the trolley?

Some would say that averting the trolley away from Einstein is the "right" choice, saving him and allowing him to live and inevitably offer the tremendous insights that he was destined to provide (we are assuming in this scenario that it is a younger adult moment-in-time, Einstein).

Not so fast, some might say, and they wonder whether the other adult, the one on the straight-ahead, maybe they are someone that is destined to be equally great or perhaps make even more notable contributions to society (who's to know?).

Anyway, I think you can see how the ethical dilemmas can be readily postulated with the Trolley Problem template.

Usually, the popular variants involve the number of people that are stuck on the tracks. For example, assume there are two people trapped on the straight-ahead path, while only one person is jammed on the forked path.

Some would say this is an "easy" answered variant since the aspect of two people is presumed to be spared over just saving one person. In that sense, you are willing to consider that lives are somewhat additive, and the more there are, the more ethically favorable is that particular choice.

Not everyone would concur with that logic.

In any case, we now have placed on the table herein the crux of the Trolley Problem.

I realize that your initial reaction likely is that it is a mildly interesting and thought-provoking notion but seems overly abstract and does not offer any practical utility.

Some object and point out that they do not envision themselves ever coming upon a trolley and perchance finding themselves in this kind of obtuse pickle.

Shift gears.

A firefighter has rushed up to a burning building.

There is a man in the building that is poking out of a window, acrid smoke billowing around him, and yelling to be saved.

What should the firefighter do?

Well, of course, we would hope that the firefighter would seek to rescue the man.

But, wait, there is the sound of a child, screaming uncontrollably, stuck in a bedroom inside the burning building.

The firefighter has to choose which to try and rescue, and for which the firefighter will not have time to save both of them.

If the firefighter chooses to save the child, the man will perish in the fire. If the firefighter chooses to save the man, the child will succumb to the fire.

Does this seem familiar?

It should because it is roughly equivalent to the Trolley Problem.

The point is that there are potentially real-life related scenarios that exhibit the underlying parameters and the overarching premise of the Trolley Problem.

Remove the trolley from the problem as stated and look at the structure or elements that underpin the circumstances (we can still refer to the matter as the Trolley Problem for sake of reference, yet remove the trolley and still retain the core essentials).

We have this:

- There are dire circumstances of a life-or-death nature (more like death-or-death)
- All outcomes are horrific (even the do-nothing option) and lead to fatality
- Time is short and there are urgency and immediacy involved
- Options are extremely limited, and a forced-choice is required

You might try to argue that there is not a "forced choice" since there is the do-nothing option always available in these scenarios, but we are going to assume that the person faced with the predicament is aware of what is taking place and realizes they are making a choice even if they choose to do nothing.

Obviously, if the person confronted with the choice is unaware of the ramifications of doing nothing, they perhaps could be said to have not been cognizant of the fact that they tacitly made a choice. Likewise, someone that miscomprehends the situation might falsely believe that they do not have to make a choice.

Assume that the person involved is fully aware of the do-nothing and must choose to do nothing or to not do-nothing (I emphasize this due to the aspect that sometimes people mulling over the Trolley Problem will attempt to weasel out of the setup by saying that the do-nothing is the "right" choice since they then have averted making any decision; the selection of do-nothing is in fact considered a decision in this setup).

As an aside, in the case of the burning building, if the firefighter does nothing, presumably both the man and the child will die, so this is somewhat kilter of the Trolley Problem as presented, thus, it is perhaps more evidentiary that the firefighter will almost certainly make a choice. It differs from the classic Trolley Problem in that the firefighter has the opportunity to always, later on, point out that the do-nothing was certainly worse than making a choice, no matter which apparent choice was ultimately selected.

One other point, this is not particularly a so-called Hobson's choice scenario, which sometimes is misleadingly likened to the Trolley Problem.

Hobson's choice is based on an historic story of a horse owner that told those wanting a horse that they could choose either the horse closest to the barn door or take no horse at all. As such, the upside is taking the horse as proffered, while the downside is that you end-up without getting a horse.

This is a decision-making scenario of a take-it-or-leave-it style, and decidedly not the same as the Trolley Problem.

With all of the background setting the stage, we can next consider how this seems to be an issue related to self-driving cars.

The focus will be on AI-based true self-driving cars, which deserves clarity as to what that phrasing means.

The Role of AI-Based Self-Driving Cars

True self-driving cars are ones that the AI drives the car entirely on its own and there isn't any human assistance during the driving task.

These driverless vehicles are considered a Level 4 and Level 5, while a car that requires a human driver to co-share the driving effort is usually considered at a Level 2 or Level 3. The cars that co-share the driving task are described as being semi-autonomous, and typically contain a variety of automated add-on's that are referred to as ADAS (Advanced Driver-Assistance Systems).

There is not yet a true self-driving car at Level 5, which we don't yet even know if this will be possible to achieve, and nor how long it will take to get there.

Meanwhile, the Level 4 efforts are gradually trying to get some traction by undergoing very narrow and selective public roadway trials, though there is controversy over whether this testing should be allowed per se (we are all life-or-death guinea pigs in an experiment taking place on our highways and byways, some point out).

Since semi-autonomous cars require a human driver, the adoption of those types of cars won't be markedly different than driving conventional vehicles, so there's not much new per se to cover about them on this topic (though, as you'll see in a moment, the points next made are generally applicable).

For semi-autonomous cars, it is important that the public needs to be forewarned about a disturbing aspect that's been arising lately, namely that in spite of those human drivers that keep posting videos of themselves falling asleep at the wheel of a Level 2 or Level 3 car, we all need to avoid being misled into believing that the driver can take away their attention from the driving task while driving a semi-autonomous car.

You are the responsible party for the driving actions of the vehicle, regardless of how much automation might be tossed into a Level 2 or Level 3.

Self-Driving Cars And The Trolley Problem

For Level 4 and Level 5 true self-driving vehicles, there won't be a human driver involved in the driving task.

All occupants will be passengers.

The AI is doing the driving.

Here's the vexing question: *Will the AI of true self-driving cars have to make Trolley Problem decisions during the act of driving the self-driving vehicle?*

The reaction by some insiders is that this is a preposterous idea and utterly miscast, labeling the whole matter as falsehood and something that has no bearing on self-driving cars.

Really?

Start with the first premise that is usually given, which is that there is no such thing as a Trolley Problem in the act of driving a car.

For anyone trying to use the "never happens" argument (for nearly anything), they find themselves on rather shaky and porous ground, since all it takes is the showing of existence to prove that the "never" is an incorrect statement.

I can easily provide that existence proof.

Peruse the news about car crashes, and by doing so, here's an example of a recent news headline from even just a week ago or so: "Driver who hit pedestrians on sidewalk was veering to avoid crash."

The real-world reporting indicated that a driver was confronted with a pick-up truck that unexpectedly pulled in front of him, and he found himself having to choose whether to ram into the other vehicle or to try and veer away from the vehicle, though he also realized apparently that there were nearby pedestrians and his veering would take him into the pedestrians.

Which to choose?

I trust that you can see that this is very much like the Trolley Problem.

If he opted to do nothing, he was presumably going to ram into the other vehicle. If he veered away, he was presumably going to potentially hit the pedestrians. Either choice is certainly terrible, yet a choice had to be made.

Some of you might bellow that this is not a life-or-death choice, and indeed fortunately the pedestrians though injured were not actually killed (at least as stated in the reporting), but I think you are fighting a bit hard to try and reject the Trolley Problem.

It can be readily argued that death was on the line.

Anyone of an open mind would agree that there was a horrific choice to be made, involving dire circumstances, and with limited choices, involving a time urgency factor, and otherwise conformed with the Trolley Problem overall (minus the trolley).

As such, for those in the "never happens" camp, this is one example, of many, for which the word never is blatantly wrong.

It does happen.

In fact, it is an interesting matter to try and gauge how often this kind of decision making does take place while driving a car. In the United States alone, there are 3.2 trillion miles driven each year, doing so by about 225 million licensed drivers, and the result is approximately 40,000 deaths and 2.3 million injuries due to car crashes annually.

We do not know how many of those crashes involved a Trolley Problem scenario, but we do know that reportedly it does occur (as evidenced by news reporting).

On that aspect of reporting, it is quite interesting that apparently, we should be cautious in interpreting any of the stories and coverage of car crashes, due to a suggested bias by such reporting.

A study discussed in the Columbia Journalism Review points out that oftentimes the driver is quoted by news reporters, rather than quoting the victims that are harmed by the driving act (this is logically explainable, since the victims are either hard to reach as they are at a hospital and possibly incapacitated, or, sadly, they are dead and thus unable to explain what happened).

You might recognize this kind of selective attention as the survivability bias, a type of everyday bias in which we tend to focus on that which is more readily available and neglect or underplay that which is less so available or apparent.

For the driving of a car and the reporting of car crashes, we need to be mindful of this facet.

It could be that there are instances involving the Trolley Problem that the surviving participants might not realize had occurred, or are reluctant to state as so, and so on. In that sense, it could be that the Trolley Problem in car crashes is underreported.

Being fair, we can also question the veracity of those that make a claim that amounts to a Trolley Problem and be cautious in assuming that just because someone says it was, it might not have been. In that sense, we could be mindful of potential overreporting.

All in all, though, we can reasonably reject the claim that the Trolley Problem does not exist in the act of driving a car.

Stated more affirmatively, *we can reasonably accept and acknowledge that the Trolley Problem does exist in the act of driving a car.*

There, I said it, and I'm sure there are some pundits that are boiling mad thereof.

Self-Driving Cars And Dealing With The Trolley Problem

Anyway, with that under our belt, we hopefully might agree that human drivers can and do face the Trolley Problem.

But is it only human drivers that experience this?

One can make the assertion that an AI-based driving system, which is supposed to drive a car and do so to the same or better capability than human drivers, could very well encounter Trolley Problem situations.

Let's tackle this carefully.

First, notice that this does not suggest that only AI driving systems will encounter a Trolley Problem, which is sometimes confusion that exists.

There are those that claim the Trolley Problem will only happen to self-driving cars, but it hopefully is clear-cut that this is something that faces human drivers and we are extending that known facet to what we assume self-driving cars will encounter too.

Second, some argue that we will have only and exclusively AI-based true self-driving cars on our roadways, and as such, those vehicles will communicate and coordinate electronically via V2X (see my discussion at **this link here**), doing so in a fashion that will obviate any chance of a Trolley Problem arising.

Maybe so, but that is a Utopian-like future that we do not know will happen, and meanwhile, there is inarguably going to be a mixture of both human-driven cars and AI-driven cars, for likely a long time to come, at least decades, and we also do not know if people will ever give up their perceived "right" (it's a privilege, see my **discussion here**) about driving a car.

This is an important point that many never-Trolley proponents overlook.

Here's how they get themselves into a corner.

The oft refrain is that an AI-based self-driving car has "obviously" been poorly engineered or essentially a lousy job done by the AI developers if the vehicle ever perchance finds itself in the midst of a Trolley Problem.

Usually, these same claims are associated too with the belief that we will have zero fatalities as a result of self-driving cars.

As I have exhorted many times, zero fatalities is a zero chance.

It is a lofty goal, and a heartwarming aspiration, but nonetheless a misleading and outright false establishment of expectations.

The rub is that if a pedestrian darts into the street, and there was no forewarning of the action, and meanwhile a self-driving car is coming down the street at perhaps 35 miles per hour, the physics of stopping in-time cannot be overcome simply because the AI is driving the car.

The usual retort is that the AI would have <u>always</u> detected the pedestrian beforehand, but this is a falsehood that implies the sensors will always and perfectly be able to detect such matters, and that it will always be done the sufficiently in advanced time that the self-driving car can avoid the pedestrian.

I dare say that a child that runs out from between two parked cars is not going to offer such a chance.

We are once again into the existence proof, meaning that there are going to be circumstances whereby no matter how good the AI is, and how good the sensors are, there will still be instances of the AI not being able to avoid a car crash.

Likewise, one can argue in that same vein that the Trolley Problem will be indeed encountered by AI self-driving cars, ones that are on our public streets, and traveling amongst human drivers, and driving near to human pedestrians.

The news report about the human driver that was cut-off by a pick-up truck could absolutely happen to a self-driving car.

This seems undebatable.

If you are now of the mind that the Trolley Problem can occur and can occur too in the case of AI self-driving cars, the next aspect is what will the AI do.

Suppose the AI jams on the brakes, and slams head-on into that pick-up truck.

Did the AI consider other options?

Was the AI even considering veering to the side of the road and up onto the sidewalk (and, into the pedestrians)?

If you are a self-driving car maker or automaker, you need to very, very, very careful about what your answer is going to be.

I'll tell you why.

You might say that the AI was only programmed to do whatever was the obvious thing to do, which was to apply the brakes and attempt to slow down.

We can likely assume that the AI was proficient enough to calculate that despite the braking, it was going to ram into the pick-up truck.

So, it "knew" that a car crash was imminent.

But if you are also saying that the AI did not consider other options, including going up onto the sidewalk, this certainly seems to showcase that the AI was doing an inadequate job of driving the car, and we would have expected a human driver to try and assess alternatives to avoid the car crash.

In that sense, the AI is presumably deficient and perhaps should not be on our public roadways.

You are also opening wide your legal liability, which I have repeatedly stated is something that will ultimately be a huge exposure for the automakers and self-driving car makers (see my piece at **this link** and **this one too**).

Once self-driving cars are prevalent, and once they get into car crashes, which they will, the lawsuits are going to come flying, and there are lawyers already priming to go after those deep-pocketed billion-dollar funded makers of self-driving tech and self-driving cars.

Meanwhile, some of you might say that the AI did consider other alternatives, defending the robustness of your AI system, including that it considered going up on the sidewalk, but it then calculated that the pedestrians might be struck and so opted to stay the course and rammed instead into the pick-up truck.

Whoa, you have just admitted that the AI was entangled into a Trolley Problem scenario.

Welcome to the fold.

Conclusion

When a human driver confronts a Trolley Problem, they presumably take into account their own potential death or injury, which thusly differs from the classic Trolley Problem since the person throwing the switch for the trolley tracks is not directly imperiled (they might suffer emotional consequences, or maybe even legal repercussions, but not bodily harm).

We can reasonably assume that the AI of a self-driving car is not concerned about its own well-being (I don't want to detract from this herein discussion and take us onto a tangent, but there are some that argue we might someday ascribe human rights to AI, see my analysis at the **link here**).

In any case, the self-driving car might have passengers in it, which introduces a third element of consideration for the Trolley Problem.

This is akin to adding a third track and another fork.

The complications though somewhat extend beyond the traditional Trolley Problem since the AI must now take into account a potential joint probability or level of uncertainty, involving the facet that in the case of the pick-up truck involves the possible death or injury to the pick-up driver <u>and</u> the self-driving car passengers, versus the possible death or injury to the pedestrians <u>and</u> the self-driving car passengers.

Maybe that is the Trolley Problem on steroids.

Time for a wrap-up.

For those flat earthers that deny the existence of the Trolley Problem in the case of AI-based true self-driving cars, your head-in-the-sand perspective is not only myopic but you are going to be the easiest of the legal targets for lawsuits.

Why so?

Because it was a well-known and oft-discussed matter that the Trolley Problem exists, yet you did nothing about it and hid behind the assertion that it does not exist.

Good luck with that.

For those of you that are the rare earthers, you acknowledge that the Trolley Problem exists for self-driving cars, but argue that it is a rarity, an edge problem, a corner case.

Tell that to the people killed when your AI-based true self-driving car hits someone, doing so in that "rare" instance that will indisputably eventually arise.

Again, it is not going to hold any legal water.

Then there are the get-round-to-it earthers that acknowledge the Trolley Problem, and lament that you are so busy right now that it is low on the priority list, and pledge that one day, when time permits, you are going to deal with it.

There really is little difference between the rare earthers and the get-round-to-it earthers, and either way, they are going to have quite some explaining to do to a jury and a judge when the time comes.

Here's what the automakers and self-driving tech firms should be doing:

- Develop a sensible and explicit strategy about the Trolley Problem
- Craft a viable plan that entails the development of AI to cope with the Trolley Problem
- Undertake appropriate testing of the AI to ascertain the Trolley Problem handling
- Rollout when so readied the AI capabilities and monitor for usage
- Adjust and enhance the AI as feasible to increasingly improve Trolley Problem handling

Hopefully, this discussion will awaken the flat earthers, and nudge forward the rare earthers and the get-round-to-it earthers, urging them to put proper and appropriate attention to the Trolley Problem and sufficiently preparing their AI driving systems to cope with these life-or-death matters.

It is serious stuff.

CHAPTER 7
EVASIVE MANEUVERING AND AI SELF-DRIVING CARS

CHAPTER 7
EVASIVE MANEUVERING AND AI SELF-DRIVING CARS

A recent news story reported that a Tesla on Autopilot managed to avoid striking a deer by undertaking an aggressive maneuver of swerving to avert striking the living animal that was in the middle of a highway lane.

Thankfully, no one was injured, neither those inside the Tesla and nor was the deer struck, and we can all relish that this story had a happy ending.

What makes this story especially newsworthy involves the aspect that the evasive maneuver was conducted in a seemingly aggressive or blatantly assertive manner by Autopilot, which until now has seemingly been more subdued and unlikely to perform harsh driving actions.

Let's take a moment to consider how humans react in circumstances involving such cases, and then reflect on what we would hope that any AI-based computer driving system would do or will end-up doing in such instances

So, quick, there's a deer in the roadway up ahead, what are you going to do?

We have all encountered those scary moments when an obstruction has suddenly appeared in front of our vehicle, causing your hands to tense-up on the steering wheel as your mind races wildly to decide what action to take.

Maybe you should jam on the brakes.

But, if the distance to the upcoming object is too close, slamming on the brakes might not stop the car in time to keep from hitting what is in the way. Furthermore, depending upon the traffic behind you, sharp-edged braking could cause other cars to ram into your vehicle, either harming you and your passengers or inexorably pushing you into the very thing you were trying to avoid hitting.

Okay, instead of braking, perhaps it would be wiser to swerve the car.

Now you have to choose between swerving to the left of the object or the right of the object.

One question involves whether the swerve in either of the two directions will bring you into even more danger. Perhaps swinging to the left will force you into head-on traffic, facing a potentially injurious or death producing frontal collision. Swerving over to the right might take you to the edge of the roadway, possibly causing the car to fly into a ditch or possibly go over a cliff.

There is much more to the calculus.

The object itself needs to be assessed in many ways.

I mentioned that the obstruction in this case was a deer.

Suppose that it was a horse, or a dog, or a squirrel, would any of those variations change what evasive action you are likely to choose?

Sure, they might very well impact the mental equations as to braking versus swerving.

A squirrel might be small enough that you can take a chance and just roll atop the creature, doing so in the possibility that there is sufficient clearance to avoid harming it. And, though this might seem callous, most people would likely rate that hitting a squirrel is not quite the same ethical dilemma as hitting a deer (I realize that some would argue that they are both equally precious).

Don't forget to add the fact that the obstruction might be in motion and able to continue in motion, which also provides fodder for considering what to do.

It could be that when you opt to swerve to the left, the object scampers to the right and thus there is less need to radically go to the left because the clearance has widened. When that happens, you typically breathe a sigh of relief and are appreciative that fate dealt the hand in that manner.

Regrettably, the object might alternatively and mistakenly turn to the left, moving further into your path, although you were trying to avoid it and now the object itself is making the situation worse. This is likely to cause a curse word or two to come from your lips as you get irked at the animal for having made the wrong choice.

Yet another factor involves the size and heft of the obstruction.

A small-sized animal is going to do less destruction and endangerment to your vehicle, and though of course you would be personally devastated at having hit the creature, at least you know that you and your passengers will likely survive relatively unharmed. The problem of striking a larger beast is that besides harming the animal, there's a high chance that the action can do substantial damage to your car and simultaneously cause you to lose control of the vehicle. It could be that upon striking the animal, you lose your steering, or the physics forces the car to head into oncoming traffic or over into an embankment.

Besides considering the role of animals, the obstruction could be something inanimate, perhaps a large piece of furniture that dropped off the back of a truck and has been sitting in the lane, awaiting a car to come along and deal with it. From time-to-time, you've probably seen debris from a smashed couch or a lazy chair that was struck by other traffic and step-by-step dashed into tons of bits and pieces.

An inanimate object does not necessarily need to be standing still.

I've seen with my own eyes an instance of a wheelchair that was slowly rolling back-and-forth on a freeway, being narrowly struck by passing cars, and upon each near strike, the wheelchair would suddenly and erratically roll in one direction or another.

All in all, whenever there is something in the roadway up ahead, and you need to consider what to do, there is a complex series of mental contortions that need to be undertaken.

The rub is that this needs to be mentally worked-out in split seconds.

Unless you are lucky enough to spy something in the roadway with a great deal of distance, usually there is very little time to consider the multitude of options, and you are forced into a nearly instantaneous selection of what to do.

You can be caught so completely off-guard that in essence, you do not decide, merely ramming directly into the obstruction.

The act of striking the obstruction might also be a deliberately derived approach, based on weighing all the factors and reaching the conclusion that the least dangerous way to cope involves proceeding unabated and hope for the best.

Why take you through all the agony and angst of what human drivers have to endure when driving a car?

Because we are gradually having AI-based driving systems that are going to be making the same kinds of choices.

Do you know how your AI-based driving system is making these types of arduous and life deciding selections?

Probably not.

There aren't automakers and self-driving tech firms revealing the proprietary means that their software arrives at such decisions.

As a human inside such vehicles, you are assuming that whatever the automation is going to do will be the "right" choice.

Of course, you are betting your life on that assumption.

It is quite a high stakes bet on something that you have no idea about how it is being calculated and whether all factors are being considered, or perhaps the approach is extremely simplistic and only has one factor or two that come into consideration.

Along those lines, realize too that for any given situation, there is not necessarily only one way to proceed.

Each of the choices involves probabilities and uncertainties, which is confounding to human drivers, and likewise if being used by the AI-based driving systems requires assessing the chances of what might occur and what might result (for more on uncertainties while driving, see my analysis at this **link here**).

If you are driving, you might assess that say if a deer is walking across the lane from left to right and already in-motion, the probability that the deer will continue in that path is presumably relatively strong. You do not know that to a one-hundred percent certainty. It is a presumed best guess.

The reality could turn out that the deer hadn't yet noticed the car, and upon realizing that the car is bearing down toward it, the deer reactively tries to retreat to whence it came, thus it turns to the left and tries to dash back in that direction.

Thus, your initial guess about the deer continuing to the right was incorrect.

Upon your detecting that the deer is now motioning to the left, you might recalibrate your choices, and even if you had already started to swerve left, maybe you now change your mind and opt to switch over to aiming to the right of the deer.

This is an intricate dance that involves a real-time reassessment of the factors and either large-scale adjustments or micro-adjustments about the heading of the car, the speed of the car, and the like.

Throughout all of this, you are somewhat shaping your choices by how radical an action you are willing to take.

Novice drivers are often timid in these situations and are fearful of possibly rolling the car or otherwise not sure how the car will react when making dramatic inflections in steering or braking. The opposite can be true too, namely, some novices do not realize that a sharp twist of the steering wheel while at high speeds could cause the car to become unstable, and so the novice unknowingly puts the vehicle into possibly greater danger than via taking more measured action.

Returning to the AI-based driving systems, consider what you want such a driving system to do.

Would you prefer that the automation select a radical maneuver, which might have advantages and also disadvantages, or take a more muted approach, which also will have its advantages and disadvantages?

Undoubtedly, some people would say that if they were a passenger in such a vehicle, they would want the AI to select only the seemingly milder maneuver rather than risking the overall safety of the entire car and its occupants, while other people might insist that radical maneuvers are fine as a means to hopefully increase the odds of avoiding striking the obstruction.

This all turns out to be more than a mathematical exercise as it involves ethical decisions that humans seem to make almost subconsciously, and yet we do make those decisions, every day that we are on the roads and driving a car.

The public-at-large has not yet especially considered the AI Ethics aspects of how AI systems are making potential life-and-death decisions involving us, though this serious matter has gradually been surfacing in other ways, such as the recent qualms about AI-based facial recognition systems that might have embedded racial bias and the same for more mundane AI like a system that decides whether to grant someone a car loan or not (for my discussion about AI Ethics, see the **link here**).

For the use case of AI-based driving systems, we are heading to a moment in time that will determine how the public and regulators are going to cope with self-driving that makes crucial real-time decisions, and for which none of us might know what method or approach is being used.

Some say they don't care how the cars do it, just as long as there are no car crashes and no human injuries or deaths.

The notion of zero fatalities for self-driving cars is farfetched and completely misleading and outright false, as I have repeatedly exhorted (see my indication that zero fatalities are a zero chance, at this **link here**), and we must all realize that the physics involved in the motion of multi-ton cars is not going to lend itself to always averting a car crash.

A deer that pops out of the bushes and surprisingly comes onto a highway lane, while a car is moving at 65 miles per hour, and if the distance is just a few feet, there is no chance of swerving or stopping to prevent hitting the deer.

And, not wanting to seem overly doom and gloom, if that was a human that decided to step onto the highway, they too would be in a bad way, regardless that the circumstance involved a human instead of a deer.

Here's a question to ponder: *Do we want AI-based true self-driving cars to be making radical driving maneuvers or do we want something more modest, and if so, who decides this?*

Let's unpack the matter and see.

Understanding The Levels Of Self-Driving Cars

As a clarification, true self-driving cars are ones that the AI drives the car entirely on its own and there isn't any human assistance during the driving task.

These driverless vehicles are considered a Level 4 and Level 5 (see my explanation at **this link here**), while a car that requires a human driver to co-share the driving effort is usually considered at a Level 2 or Level 3. The cars that co-share the driving task are described as being semi-autonomous, and typically contain a variety of automated add-on's that are referred to as ADAS (Advanced Driver-Assistance Systems).

There is not yet a true self-driving car at Level 5, which we don't yet even know if this will be possible to achieve, and nor how long it will take to get there. Meanwhile, the Level 4 efforts are gradually trying to get some traction by undergoing very narrow and selective public roadway trials, though there is controversy over whether this testing should be allowed per se (we are all life-or-death guinea pigs in an experiment taking place on our highways and byways, some point out).

Since semi-autonomous cars require a human driver, the adoption of those types of cars won't be markedly different than driving conventional vehicles, so there's not much new per se to cover about them on this topic (though, as you'll see in a moment, the points next made are generally applicable).

For semi-autonomous cars, it is important that the public needs to be forewarned about a disturbing aspect that's been arising lately, namely that despite those human drivers that keep posting videos of themselves falling asleep at the wheel of a Level 2 or Level 3 car, we all need to avoid being misled into believing that the driver can take away their attention from the driving task while driving a semi-autonomous car.

You are the responsible party for the driving actions of the vehicle, regardless of how much automation might be tossed into a Level 2 or Level 3.

Self-Driving Cars And Maneuvering

For a Level 2 or Level 3 car (a Tesla on Autopilot is currently considered a Level 2), one of the greatest concerns for these types of semi-autonomous vehicles is that the human and the automation might end-up at odds with each other when making driving choices.

As earlier pointed out about deciding what to do about a deer in the roadway, the automation might ascertain that swerving is the maneuver to undertake, and yet suppose the human driver at the wheel believes it is better to not swerve and instead brake, or perhaps just proceed ahead and possibly strike the animal.

The usual answer is that if the human driver wants to do something else, all they need to do is override the automation.

That seems to solve any questions on this matter.

Unfortunately, this simplistic and rather flippant answer does not solve things.

Imagine that the automation has already begun to swerve to the left. The human driver now has a much different situation than they did a split second earlier. The car is already now amid a choice that the human driver did not make and presumably (we are assuming for the moment) believed was unwise.

This is what happens when you co-share the driving task.

It is akin to having another driver sitting next to you that has full access to the driving controls. When split-second decisions need to be made, you do not have time to chat with each other about what choice is best. Instead, each of you is going to make a rather instantaneous choice.

The problem then becomes that one of you engages their choice, and the other has not yet done so, but now that the other one began their choice, it puts the other driver into a further pickle.

Anyone that says the human driver can merely takeover the controls is not being realistic about those split-second life-or-death moments that arise when driving a car. There are of course lots of situations whereby there might be enough time to have the human overrule the automation and take a course of action, yet this does not mean and nor imply that such ample opportunity will always be the case.

Consider too how the automation is making these choices.

We don't know since Tesla and likewise, other automakers are not revealing their approaches being used.

It could be a straightforward mathematical equation, and if so, what factors are being used?

How does the equation figure out the odds of striking versus not striking the obstruction, and what about the risks of the maneuver in terms of subtle versus radical, and what about the value associated with those inside the car versus the animal, and so on.

Some argue that we should just let the Machine Learning (ML) and Deep Learning (DL) determine what to do.

The use of ML/DL is a computational pattern matching mechanism that uses past data to try and find patterns that can be invoked for making later decisions. If we fed lots of instances of evasive maneuvers, the pattern matching would try to calculate how to react to future such occasions.

Do not be misled into believing that ML/DL solves the matter since the nature of the data and cases used to train the ML/DL might create a false semblance of what to do (often using large datasets that are fed into an artificial neural network).

Suppose that most or all prior instances were "solved" via the act of braking, then the calculations would statistically tend toward using braking in future situations. There isn't any kind of common-sense reasoning involved by the automation.

Conclusion

If indeed the Tesla Autopilot is getting more aggressive in evasive maneuvers, we should be wondering why.

For example:

- Has the use of ML/DL led the Autopilot to gradually over time mathematically calculate that using a radial maneuver is best?

- In all cases or only in certain kinds of situations?

- Are the AI developers and engineers that have devised the Autopilot opting to ratchet up the radical maneuver facet, and if so, what kind of testing and to what degree is this a safer method of driving?

The usual answer for Tesla and other Level 2 and Level 3 providers is that it doesn't matter what the automation does since the human driver is the final arbitrator and fully responsible for the driving of the car.

Though that seems perhaps "sensible" on the surface, we will undoubtedly eventually find out via our legal system and lawsuits entailing injuries and deaths involving Level 2 and Level 3 cars as to whether this kind of shifting of the blame can be societally acceptable (for my predictions about such lawsuits).

We need to have a more open dialogue about how such driving systems work and stop pretending that some behind-the-scenes Wizard of Oz is magically taking care of things for us.

But maybe that kind of dialoguing is too radical of an idea for some.

CHAPTER 8

MOVIE MISCASTING AI AND AI SELF-DRIVING CARS

CHAPTER 8
MOVIE MISCASTING AI AND AI SELF-DRIVING CARS

A recent news story shaking up Hollywood involves the reported casting of a robot to be the star of a $70 million budgeted science fiction movie.

You might be puzzled as to why any undue notice would come from opting to use a robot in a sci-fi movie, which has otherwise seemingly been the case for decades.

Here's the twist.

The backers of the film are alleging that the robot will use AI and essentially act or perform in the same manner that a human actor might do so, thus, in their estimation, this will be the first time that a movie starred an artificially intelligent actor.

It is claimed that the robot has been "taught" how to act and embraces the revered approach known as method acting.

So, just to clarify, this is not a CGI kind of movie editing that will showcase the robot, and nor will the robot have a human hiding inside it or have a handler sitting off-camera with a remote control. Supposedly the robot will be using its embodied AI and acting through the use of voice and body-like movements, entirely on its own.

For all of you aspiring actors, if you weren't already worried about the bleakness of landing an acting job, note that once those AI-based robots become part of the SCAG (Screen Actors Guild) and begin auditioning for juicy roles on film and TV, you are going to become even more despondent about your chosen career path.

Imagine coming home after a grueling audition for a part in a new series, and upon being asked by a close friend about how it went, for which you then grumble that a darned robot seemed to win over the producer and director and you lamentedly have once again lost an acting gig to one of those robot-turned-actor androids.

Curse the robots!

In the case of this still being planned out sci-fi movie, the robot is considered a female, at least as stated by the filmmakers, and so the headlines are saying that the robot is the starring actress in the film.

Also, the robot has been given a name, Erica.

How do we know the robot is a female?

Because the robot maker says so, and since the robot has been given a facial look resembling a woman and the voice and mannerisms programmed into the robot are akin to what is considered a female (per the views of those making the movie).

If you are wondering whether the gender aspects go any deeper, it seems quite unlikely.

Of course, one obvious and immediate criticism is that this "female" that is an "actress" will be portraying whatever stereotypical assumptions that the robot maker and those involved in the film have about the nature of women and femininity.

That alone is worthy of concern.

There are many more concerns to pile onto this notion of a so-called artificially intelligent actor or actress.

From an AI perspective, the whole thing stinks and reeks of hogwash, unfortunately.

How so?

Where this appears to be headed involves the moviemaker suggesting or even outright claiming that the AI instills the same thinking processes and capabilities as that of humans, in essence as though the AI has become sentient (for my explanation about AI and sentience, see the **link here**).

Please know this: *There isn't any AI today that is sentient, and no such AI is on the horizon, therefore any news or media that attempt to say otherwise is erroneously perpetuating an untoward myth and falsehood.*

You might be tempted to shrug off any of the reports that allude to AI as being the equivalent of human thinking and see this as just idle fun and not a serious matter.

The danger with these attempts at anthropomorphizing today's AI is that it can cause the public to believe that AI can do things it cannot do, and in that belief can get people into trouble by assuming that the AI will carry out activities in a human-like contemplative manner.

Do not fall for that fakery.

This is why the idea of a well-budgeted movie opting to try and foster the charade of AI as equivalent to human capabilities is summarily worrisome and downright troubling.

If the movie gets a strong box office upon being finished and released, the movie and its presumed marketing campaign are likely to further reinforce the outlandishness of what AI is. People watching the film might fall hook, line, and sinker into believing what they see.

Anyone serious about AI will maybe at first be excited to have such attention being brought to AI, though this initial elation by AI developers will get sober real quickly when they are asked to proffer AI that can do things that only humans can do today.

Oops, the realization of limits to what AI can do will hit the proverbial fan.

In short, despite the allusion of casting an AI-based robot that seemingly can act and perform on its own, this is really still a programmed artifice that has no semblance of human intelligence and merely represents various trickery to seem human-like.

Ways To Create AI False Impressions

The robot named as Erica is known amongst AI insiders and has been around for several years as an ongoing research project.

From time-to-time, the robot has gotten some splashy stories written about what it does.

The problem with most of those showy stories is that they are often written by someone that has absolutely no clue of what AI is, nor how robots work, and thusly the writer tends to gush and become enamored that the final breakthrough in AI and robotics has arrived (which, they have no idea as to how to make such a judgment or proclamation).

It can be difficult to discern if those writers are naïve, or simply want to believe, or maybe are doing a wink-wink tall tale, or what they have in mind.

The most beguiling instances involve the writer being handed a script, containing pre-determined questions to ask the AI-based robot, and the writer does so, willingly and without questioning the appropriateness of such an approach to doing an "interview" or any semblance of investigative reporting.

We are all used to the advances in Natural Language Processing (NLP) that have emerged in the last several years, as evidenced by the popularity of Alexa, Siri, and the like. At first, people unfamiliar with modern-day NLP were shocked to discover that those NLP systems seemed to be responsive to verbal commands.

Anybody that has tried using those NLP systems for any length of time and for any kind of demanding dialogue is now of the realization that despite the great advances so far, the AI NLP is still a far cry from being the same conversationalist as humans are (indeed, there is a tremendous amount of research on conversational AI, attempting to push forward on those capabilities).

If someone hands you a script of questions, and you ask those questions of an AI system, you do not have to be a rocket scientist to guess that the NLP will respond with potentially human-like answers, due to being programmed beforehand to do so.

The moment you veer from the script, it becomes possible to begin to detect the boundaries of what the AI can do. It might keep up briefly, and then as you get deeper into what would be an everyday discussion with a human, gradually the AI will falter in terms of remaining as a seemingly engaging discussant.

You might be interested in knowing some of the tricks of the trade that are used to create an impression that the AI NLP is human or has human-like abilities.

One approach is to have the NLP utter vocal fillers, such as saying "uhuh" or "ok" that a human might do when you are talking. This gives you the feeling that the AI is actively listening to you, but it is more of a gimmick rather than a semblance of understanding or comprehension.

Another handy tool is to use fallback utterances when needed.

Let's imagine that you have stated a lengthy comment and the AI NLP has no clue what you stated, not having been able to parse the words and try and find some aligned response. In that case, rather than directly and honestly stating that the system does not grasp what you have said, which obviously is a giveaway that the AI NLP is weak, the reply instead would be something like "very interesting" or "tell me more."

The beauty of those fallback utterances is that you will tend to think that the AI NLP did comprehend what you said and is engaged and desirous of further discussion.

Parroting is also a handy means to fool someone.

If a human says to the AI that they are tired, the reply can be simply crafted as "tell me why you are tired" and the human then thinks that the AI is being sympathetic and understood the discourse (there isn't any kind of common-sense reasoning yet in today's AI, and a long ways to go to get there, see my discussion at this **link here**).

The icing on the cake involves the addition of seemingly emotional actions such as offering a laugh or maybe a sigh, all of which appear to be human-like responses. This though can be a dual-edged sword in that if the AI NLP vocalizes laughter, but you have not said something presumably funny, it can potentially reveal that the canned laughter is insincere and break the veneer of being human.

You might find of interest a famous concept referred to as the uncanny valley.

It is a theory that as an AI-based robot proceeds from being an obvious robot toward appearing to be human, there will be a juncture at which the appearance begins to evoke repulsion from a human interacting with the robot. Seemingly, when you can readily discern that a robot is merely a robot, you are tolerant and willing to interact, but when it begins to get overly close to human-like behavior, the result seems creepy.

In that sense, the AI robot falls into a "valley" in terms of your feelings toward the system, and the only way out would be for it to retreat to its former lesser self, or climb out by leaping all the way to becoming indistinguishable from a human.

Not everyone agrees that this uncanny valley proposition is valid, though it does provide interesting fodder for considering how to best deploy an AI-based robotic system.

I'll briefly bring up another facet that you might find of interest about AI.

Within the AI field, there is a kind of test known as the Turing Test. The notion involves having an AI system be behind say a curtain, hidden from view, and have a human likewise behind another curtain, and a moderator begins asking them both various questions. If the moderator cannot distinguish between the two as to which is the AI and which is the human, presumably the AI has successfully demonstrated the equivalent of human intelligence and passed a test that attempts to make that assessment (the test is named by its inventor, the famous mathematician Alan Turing).

At first glance, the Turing Test seems perfectly sensible.

There are some potential problems.

Perhaps the biggest problem is associated with the moderator. If the moderator does a lousy job of asking questions and engaging the hidden contestants, the nature and scope of the interaction might be insufficient to properly make a judgment about which is which.

This is the same as my earlier point about those writers or reporters that go along with a predetermined script. In that sense, they are somewhat a "moderator" in conducting a test of the AI, yet they are sticking with a preset series of questions.

Keep in mind too that most of the AI NLP systems have a human-machine dialogue corpus, meaning a database that employs various AI techniques, and once you go beyond that established base, there is a degradation in what the AI NLP can do.

When you want to try and figure out how shallow or deep an AI NLP might be, the easiest means is to jump all around in terms of the knowledge areas involved, gauging what the boundaries are of the system.

Please do not misinterpret my remarks as though the use of AI NLP is somehow wrong or to be avoided.

There are lots of helpful uses for AI NLP and it should be heralded for what it can do.

Maybe you've used some of the latest AI NLP to prepare yourself for a job interview, or in the case of senior citizens, the AI NLP can be an easy means to operate appliances throughout their home. Chatbots have rapidly sprung up in online use for filling out a car loan application and similar automated assistance is occurring via NLP.

The problem becomes when the AI is portrayed as being more embellished and more capable than it truly is.

The rising interest in AI Ethics has been partially sparked by farfetched claims made by AI developers and those fielding AI systems that are overeager to depict their AI as being human-like when it is not that way at all.

Seeking to improve AI NLP and robots toward the laudable goal of being human-like is fine and encouraged, but the results need to be shared with the public in a manner that offers needed caveats and overtly listed limits of what the technology can do.

In terms of the robot Erica that supposedly used "method acting" to perfect its craft, such a claim would undoubtedly cause Konstantin Stanislavski to turnover in his grave (he is a famous Russian theatre practitioner known for *The Method* of acting). In brief, the techniques involve a human actor finding their inner motives, intermingling their conscious and subconscious thoughts.

Trying to assert that any of today's AI was able to do the same is not only hyperbole, but it also denigrates the substance of what method acting has become and how it works.

But that's just par for the course when AI is oftentimes portrayed in hyperbolic ways.

Consider for a moment other areas in which AI is sometimes being inappropriately portrayed, such as the advent of true self-driving cars.

Let's unpack the matter and see.

Understanding The Levels Of Self-Driving Cars

As a clarification, true self-driving cars are ones that the AI drives the car entirely on its own and there isn't any human assistance during the driving task.

These driverless vehicles are considered a Level 4 and Level 5, while a car that requires a human driver to co-share the driving effort is usually considered at a Level 2 or Level 3. The cars that co-share the driving task are described as being semi-autonomous, and typically contain a variety of automated add-on's that are referred to as ADAS (Advanced Driver-Assistance Systems).

There is not yet a true self-driving car at Level 5, which we don't yet even know if this will be possible to achieve, and nor how long it will take to get there.

Meanwhile, the Level 4 efforts are gradually trying to get some traction by undergoing very narrow and selective public roadway trials, though there is controversy over whether this testing should be allowed per se (we are all life-or-death guinea pigs in an experiment taking place on our highways and byways).

Since semi-autonomous cars require a human driver, the adoption of those types of cars won't be markedly different than driving conventional vehicles, so there's not much new per se to cover about them on this topic (though, as you'll see in a moment, the points next made are generally applicable).

For semi-autonomous cars, it is important that the public needs to be forewarned about a disturbing aspect that's been arising lately, namely that despite those human drivers that keep posting videos of themselves falling asleep at the wheel of a Level 2 or Level 3 car, we all need to avoid being misled into believing that the driver can take away their attention from the driving task while driving a semi-autonomous car.

You are the responsible party for the driving actions of the vehicle, regardless of how much automation might be tossed into a Level 2 or Level 3.

Self-Driving Cars And AI Allusions

Returning to the points about AI potentially being misstated in terms of capabilities, there are plentiful examples in the self-driving car realm.

One that was just described consists of Level 2 and Level 3 cars, whereby some automakers and self-driving tech firms overstate or tend to imply that the semi-autonomous system can do more than it can.

And, for those of you that were doubtful about whether AI misrepresentations are important or serious, note that in the case of driving a car, this is a very serious business consisting of life-or-death consequences.

A human driver that does not understand the limits of the AI that is co-sharing the driving task is bound to end-up in dicey situations and get themselves injured or killed, along with any passengers and others that might be nearby when a car crash occurs.

In the case of Level 4 and Level 5, there will not be a human driver at the wheel, and thus the issue of co-sharing the driving is obviated.

That being said, just because an automaker or self-driving tech firm claims they have AI that can properly and safely drive a car does not mean that we should take them at their word. Having a true self-driving car roaming our streets entails a multi-ton vehicle that can do tremendous damage and destruction if it is not ready to be driving solo.

Conclusion

The problem with the sci-fi movie and its apparent effort to exaggerate the capabilities of AI are that this can spill over into other areas of AI usage.

Perhaps someone that watches the movie will become bolder with their Level 2 and Level 3 car, believing from the film that AI everywhere is magically capable and sentient, and therefore it is acceptable to be less attentive to the driving task.

That would be a shame (or worse) and turn what should have been an escapist sci-fi into a real-world catastrophe.

Don't believe everything you see and especially be doubtful when today's AI starts talking or acting as though it can think like a human, which I assure is nothing more than a form of programmatic method acting, whereby some nifty AI techniques are trying to take on an acting role as humans, despite not being anywhere near to human capacities and performing outside of their league.

The well-known actor Sanford Meisner, the creator of the Meisner acting technique, had famously said that "Acting is behaving truthfully under imaginary circumstances."

I believe that we want AI that behaves truthfully under real-world circumstances.

Cut and print.

CHAPTER 9
SNAKES IN A CAR AND AI SELF-DRIVING CARS

CHAPTER 9

SNAKES IN A CAR AND AI SELF-DRIVING CARS

Just about everyone has heard of the famous movie *Snakes On A Plane*.

Having been released in 2006 to great fanfare, the movie has become a cult classic, along with being exceedingly parodied and has spawned an endless spate of online memes.

You might also be familiar with the line expressed by Samuel L. Jackson when his character has had just about enough of those darned snakes, of which the cleaned-up version of the line that was used in the film as edited for TV broadcasting was this: "I have had it with these monkey-fighting snakes on this Monday-to-Friday plane!"

For those of you that know the original line, go ahead and substitute the words accordingly (or, if you are unaware of the actual words utilized, a quick search via the Internet can readily reveal the true wording, though be ready for what you will see).

Snakes are certainly not confined to invading airplanes, which of course is a rarity and the movie proffers a rather wild premise for how the snakes got there (I don't want to reveal a significant plot point and possibly spoil the movie for you).

Snakes have also been known to find their way into cars.

Incidents of snakes in cars have been reported in Florida from time-to-time. This seems eminently sensible since we might readily expect snakes to exist there and warnings aplenty are posted throughout the Sunshine State to be wary of potential poisonous snakes. When cases arise in places such as Kansas and Oklahoma, you can usually bet that it was a pet snake that got loose or some other oddity that arose.

The latest such headline report about a snake in a car involved a man in Australia that was surprised to discover a snake crawling up his leg, doing so as he was driving at top speeds on a major highway.

Imagine that your hands are on the steering wheel and you are calmly driving along at 60 mph when all of a sudden you feel something on your legs.

Not wanting to be distracted from the roadway, you likely do a furtive glance down to see what it is.

When you realize it is a slithering snake, I'm not sure any of us would have the presence of mind to safely drive the vehicle and fend off the snake at the same time.

In those harrowing moments, the snake started to wrap around the man's legs tightly, and then the head of the snaked began to strike, hitting the driver's seat, directly between the man's legs.

Now that's scary.

Furthermore, it was an eastern brown snake and later confirmed to be one of the deadliest venom-producing snakes alive.

What did the man do?

Luckily, he had a knife within reach and used it to stab at the snake, along with using his seatbelt to entangle the snake.

The end score: Man scores a 1, snake scores a 0.

He was able to kill the snake and thus lived to tell the tale of the time that a vicious snake got into his car.

A police car came to find out what had happened and the cop recorded a video of the discussion with the man about the incident. Paramedics arrived and ascertained that the man had not been bitten, though he was in quite a state of overall shock about the traumatic experience.

Would you be able to drive home at that point?

One thing seems for sure, you would double-check, or perhaps even triple-check the vehicle to make sure that no other snakes were going along for a ride.

Though we might at first glimpse consider the story to be nothing more than some idle lighthearted news that perchance had a happy ending, there is more substance that can be gleaned from this otherwise innocuous incident.

How so?

Allow me to explain.

We are gradually heading toward the advent of AI-based true self-driving cars.

It is hoped that via self-driving cars there will be a lot fewer car crashes, and thus many fewer injuries and fatalities due to our use of cars.

The belief is that the AI will be able to drive properly, avoiding the foibles of human driving, including that human drivers at times get on-the-road while intoxicated and sadly get into untoward results (an estimated one-third of the annual car crash deaths in the United States are due to drunk drivers, see the various stats at my analysis posted at **this link here**).

Here is an intriguing question: *What might occur if you are inside a self-driving car, while the AI is doing the driving, and a snake appears?*

Since it is relatively rare for a snake to be inside a car, we'll widen the scope of the question to consider what a passenger in a self-driving car might do when encountering any kind of unexpected urgency that arises while inside a self-driving car.

Before we get to that discussion, it is important to clarify the notion of what a self-driving car consists of.

Let's unpack the matter and see.

Understanding The Levels Of Self-Driving Cars

As a clarification, true self-driving cars are ones that the AI drives the car entirely on its own and there isn't any human assistance during the driving task.

These driverless vehicles are considered a Level 4 and Level 5, while a car that requires a human driver to co-share the driving effort is usually considered at a Level 2 or Level 3. The cars that co-share the driving task are described as being semi-autonomous, and typically contain a variety of automated add-on's that are referred to as ADAS (Advanced Driver-Assistance Systems).

There is not yet a true self-driving car at Level 5, which we don't yet even know if this will be possible to achieve, and nor how long it will take to get there.

Meanwhile, the Level 4 efforts are gradually trying to get some traction by undergoing very narrow and selective public roadway trials, though there is controversy over whether this testing should be allowed per se (we are all life-or-death guinea pigs in an experiment taking place on our highways and byways, some point out).

Since semi-autonomous cars require a human driver, the adoption of those types of cars won't be markedly different than driving conventional vehicles, so there's not much new per se to cover about them on this topic (though, as you'll see in a moment, the points next made are generally applicable).

For semi-autonomous cars, it is important that the public needs to be forewarned about a disturbing aspect that's been arising lately, namely that despite those human drivers that keep posting videos of themselves falling asleep at the wheel of a Level 2 or Level 3 car, we all need to avoid being misled into believing that the driver can take away their attention from the driving task while driving a semi-autonomous car.

You are the responsible party for the driving actions of the vehicle, regardless of how much automation might be tossed into a Level 2 or Level 3.

Self-Driving Cars And Interior Threats

For Level 4 and Level 5 true self-driving vehicles, there won't be a human driver involved in the driving task.

All occupants will be passengers.

The AI is doing the driving.

Okay, so let's assume that you are quietly riding in a self-driving car, perhaps reading a book or watching a movie, and all of a sudden, a snake appears.

We can use the snake example first, and then enlarge the scope to other kinds of threats that might unexpectedly occur while inside a self-driving car.

If you are wondering how a snake can get into a car, it seems to be a lot easier than we might all imagine. Snakes are slim enough that they can sometimes enter via an exterior vent. That's rather chilling and might cause you to have nightmares, sorry, so let's agree that the odds of entry in that manner are very low.

They can come up through the undercarriage of the car, though it does not suggest they can easily make their way into the closed interior. Likewise, snakes are known to sometimes crawl into the engine space, but this too does not particularly grant them access to the inside of the vehicle.

Some believe that much of the time that a snake gets into a car is via an open window or a car door that is left open or ajar.

A person might have parked the car someplace that has snakes (let's assume the person is unaware of the presence of snakes), and upon leaving the window of the car rolled down, the snake perchance opts to check out the nice upholstery inside the vehicle. Similarly, someone might leave their car door open for a moment, stepping to the trunk to check that it is closed, and in the intervening time a snake manages to fudge its way into the car.

In whatever manner that a snake can weasel into a conventional car, we might as well assume that the same could happen with a self-driving car.

This is an important point.

For many people, they seem to think that a self-driving car is some kind of super-vehicle that is unlike any car they've ever seen or been in.

Just to set the record straight, a self-driving car is still a car. It is vulnerable in the same ways that any car might be vulnerable. No superpowers.

A self-driving car can get a flat tire. Self-driving cars can suffer mechanical breakdowns while on the highway or driving down a neighborhood street. All in all, you need to realize and anticipate that self-driving cars are going to have the same physical issues as does any regular car.

You do not hear about such aspects because today's self-driving car tryouts are being run in a carefully orchestrated way. These self-driving cars are some of the most pampered vehicles on this planet. Typically, each night, the self-driving cars are given a maintenance inspection to ensure they are ready for traveling the next day.

Once we have self-driving cars on a widespread basis, do not expect the same heightened degree of care and thus there are measurable odds that we will see self-driving cars that at times are on the side of the road, waiting to be towed or otherwise requiring being fixed, akin to today's conventional cars.

As an aside, some argue that self-driving cars should only be owned in fleets, rather than by individuals, so that the vehicles will get the proper amount of diligent attention and care. The worry is that the average person, often failing to take proper maintenance for their vehicles, will mar the use of self-driving cars if serving as an owner of such vehicles and cause the public to lose faith in using self-driving cars, precisely due to a lack of sufficient upkeep.

Anyway, we were discussing that a snake has been discovered inside a self-driving car while you are riding in the vehicle and perhaps heading to work or maybe home for the day.

What happens next?

If you are thinking that the AI is going to realize a snake is present, better think again.

Though most self-driving cars will likely have inward-facing cameras, used to detect aspects such as when riders opt to mark graffiti or rip the interior, there is little chance that the AI will be using the camera to look for snakes.

To clarify, the AI could be programmed to do so, but it just is not something of much priority. At best, it would be considered an edge or corner case. An edge or corner case is ranked as something not especially vital and that can be dealt with at a later time.

Unless we suddenly have lots of incidents of snakes in cars, there is not much incentive to try and use Machine Learning (ML) or Deep Learning (DL) to look for snakes inside a vehicle. I suppose it might be a bonus that could be used to attract people toward using a particular brand of self-driving cars. Just imagine a catchy slogan when you get to the Florida airport and want to rent a car, namely that brand X of self-driving cars will be your second pair of eyes to spot snakes that might invade your vehicle.

Would that be the pizzazz that causes you to rent that brand?

Alright, back to the snake in the self-driving car.

Since the AI is not going to likely notice the snake, it is up to you to do so.

You detect the snake.

What now?

Presumably, you have a couple of options.

One is to try and get the car to come to a halt so that you can leap out and escape the snake.

Or, maybe shove the snake out of the car, though you probably do not care if the car is moving or not and would gladly push the snake out even while speeding along.

The other possibility seems to be either to fight the snake or attempt to hide from it.

Should you tell the AI what is taking place, and if so, what would the AI do or tell you to do?

First, be aware that some of the automakers and self-driving car firms are currently imagining that the only interaction you will have with the AI is to indicate your desired destination. That's all. You tell the AI where you want to go, and until you reach your destination, there is no interaction between you and the AI.

Preposterous, I have exhorted repeatedly.

Passengers in self-driving cars are going to expect a lot more interaction with the AI. You might want to change your destination, or perhaps make a quick stop along the way of your journey. You might be hungry and seek to have the AI drive the vehicle through a McDonald's or Starbuck's. And so on.

Few journeys in a car are completely silent and entail absolutely no interaction with the driver.

You might counterargue that when you take a cab, you rarely speak with the driver. Those kinds of driving journeys are typically very short in duration. The expectation is that self-driving cars are likely to become our mainstay of travel and as such, not just a quick ride from an airport to a hotel.

Overall, there is going to be a rising expectation that the AI of the driving system must engage in a fuller semblance of a conversation with the passengers.

Assume that the AI is going to be very rudimentary for quite a while, and the Natural Language Processing (NLP) is not much more advanced than the dialogues that you have with Alex or Siri of today (I am not dinging those NLP systems, and merely pointing out that though NLP has increasingly been advancing, kudos, you would be hard-pressed to say that it is fully conversational in a robust human-like manner).

You decide to yell to the AI: "Hey, there's a snake in this darned car!"

Given that there are some smarmy wisecracks preloaded into Alexa and Siri, one supposes that an AI developer might have embedded a quip as a response, maybe something like this: "Next time, take a plane."

Bottom-line is the AI does not have any semblance of common-sense reasoning or anything approaching sentience, and it is not going to comprehend your qualms about the snake being inside the car.

Generally, you are going to need to be clearer about what you want to happen and not otherwise confound or bewilder the AI NLP.

You might instruct the AI to immediately bring the car to a halt.

Realize though that this is something that the AI will be deciding on your behalf as to how to best proceed in doing so. A human driver might radically jam on the brakes. The AI is unlikely to be programmed to do so and will instead attempt to safely and rather gingerly bring the car to a stop.

Most of the self-driving cars will have an OnStar-like connection to a remote human agent, and as such, the AI will likely connect you to the agent or you might request to be so connected. This does not especially help you in terms of fighting the snake.

You might be able to establish contact with a snake wrangler, using the in-car communications capabilities, but that is going to take time and you meanwhile are presumably going head-to-head with a potentially deadly snake.

Overall, it seems that you are going to have to try and corral the snake or use something in the vehicle to keep you separated from the snake. If perchance you have a knife or weapon, it might be used against the snake, though this is obviously a dangerous ploy too.

By potentially creating a blocking effort, you might buy time for the self-driving car to meanwhile slow down enough for you to leap out of the car. If there is a means instead to safely toss the snake out or get it to go out, presumably that would be a preferred approach.

I suppose the one piece of good news is that at least you are not driving the car.

Whereas the man in Australia had to deal with two life-threatening acts at the same time, dealing with driving the car and simultaneously battling the snake, you can fully concentrate on the snake.

Hopefully, that gives you some cheer.

Conclusion

The odds of a snake inside a self-driving car would seem rather remote.

On the other hand, having an emergency of some kind while inside a self-driving car is going to happen, and possibly occur with great frequency if we are all opting to use self-driving cars over conventional cars.

With traditional cars, there must be a human driver, and thus the human driver can potentially aid whatever emergency is arising.

In the case of self-driving cars, there isn't a human driver. Therefore, the passenger or passengers have no one else to immediately lend a hand. This is also why some are questioning whether it should be allowed to have children riding solo as passengers inside self-driving cars, doing so without adult supervision.

All told, this is an important food-for-thought discussion about our future and the arising era of self-driving cars, prompted by a seemingly oddball instance of a snake in a car.

Hey, since those snakes on a plane never had a chance when pitted against Samuel L. Jackson, maybe we ought to have an AI capability that mimics him, and thus when you are trapped in a self-driving car with a snake, you can yell out for the AI to engage the Samuel L. Jackson mode.

Undoubtedly, any snake worth its salt will know to get the heck out of there, like immediately.

CHAPTER 10

COGNITIVE TESTS AND AI SELF-DRIVING CARS

CHAPTER 10
COGNITIVE TESTS AND AI SELF-DRIVING CARS

Seems like the news recently has been filled with revelations about the taking of cognitive deficiency tests.

This is especially being widely noted by some prominent politicians that appear to be attempting to vouch for having mental clarity upon reaching an age in life whereby cognitive decline often surfaces.

Such tests are more aptly referred to as cognitive assessment tests rather than deficiency oriented tests, though the notion generally being that if a score earned is less than what might be expected, the potential conclusion is that the person has had a decline in their mental prowess.

Oftentimes also referred to as cognitive impairment detection exams, the person seeking to find out how they are mentally doing is administered a test consisting of various questions and asked to answer the questions.

The administrator of the test then "grades" the answers as to correctness and fluidity, producing a score to indicate how the person overall performed.

The score is then compared to the scores of others that have taken the test, trying to gauge how the cognitive capacity of the person is rated or ranked in light of some larger population of test-takers.

Also, if a person takes the test over time, perhaps say once per year, their prior scores are compared to their most recent score, attempting to measure whether there is a difference emerging as they age.

There are some crucial rules-of-thumb about all of this cognitive test-taking.

For example, if the person takes the same test word-for-word, repeatedly over time, this raises questions about the nature of the test versus the nature of the cognitive abilities of the person taking the test. In essence, you can potentially do better on the test simply because you've seen the same questions before and likely also had been previously told what the considered correct answers are.

One argument to be made is that this is somewhat assessing your ability to remember having previously taken the test, but that's not usually the spirit of what such cognitive tests are supposed to be about. The idea is to assess overall cognition, and not merely be focused on whether you perchance can recall the specific questions of a specific test previously taken.

Another facet of this kind of cognitive test-taking consists of being formally administered the test, rather than taking the test entirely on your own.

Though there are plenty of available cognitive tests that you can download and take in private, some would say that this is not at all the same as taking a test under the guiding hands and watch of someone certified or otherwise authorized to administer such tests.

A key basis for claiming that the test needs to be formally administered is to ensure that the person taking the test is not undermining the test or flouting the testing process. If the test taker were to ask a friend for help, this obviously defeats the purpose of the test, which is supposed to focus on your solitary cognition and not be a collective semblance of cognition. Likewise, these tests are usually timed, and a person on their own might be tempted to exceed the normally allotted time, plus the person might be tempted to look-up answers, use a calculator, etc.

Perhaps the most important reason to have a duly authorized and trained administrator involves attempting to holistically evaluate the results of the cognition test.

Experts in cognitive test-taking are quick to emphasize that a robust approach to the matter consists of not just the numeric score that a test taker achieves, but also how they are overall able to interact with a fully qualified and trained cognitive-test administrator.

Unlike taking a secured SAT or ACT test that you might have had to painstakingly sit through for college entrance purposes, a cognitive assessment test is typically intended to assess in both a written way and in a broader manner how the person interacts and cognitively presents themselves.

Imagine for example that someone aces the written test, yet meanwhile, they are unable to carry on a lucid conversation with the administrator, and similarly, they mentally stumble on why they are taking the test or otherwise have apparent cognitive difficulties surrounding the test-taking process. Those facets outside of the test itself should be counted, some would vehemently assert, and thus would be unlikely to be valued if a person merely took the test on their own.

Despite all of the foregoing and the holistic nuances that I've mentioned, admittedly, most of the time all that people want to know is what was their darned score on that vexing cognitive test.

You might be wondering whether there is one standardized and universal cognitive test that is used for these purposes.

No, there is not just one per se.

Instead, there are a bewildering and veritable plethora of such cognition tests.

It seems like each day there is some new version that gets announced to the world. In some cases, the cognitive test being proffered has been carefully prepared and analyzed for its validity. Unfortunately, in other cases, the cognitive test is a gimmick and being fronted as a moneymaker, whereby those pushing the test are aiming to get people to believe in it and hoping to generate gobs of revenue by how many take the test and charge them fees accordingly.

Please do not fall for the fly-by-night cognitive tests.

Sadly, sometimes a known celebrity or other highly visible person gets associated with a cognitive test promotion and adds a veneer of authenticity to something that does not deserve any bona fide reputational stamp-of-approval.

Some cognitive tests have lasted the test of time and are considered the dominant or at least well-regarded for their cognitive assessing capacity and validity.

On a related note, if a cognitive test takes a long time to complete, let's say hours of completion time, the odds are that it is not going to be overall well-received and considered onerous for testing purposes. As such, the "popular" cognitive tests tend to be the ones that take a relatively short period to undertake, such as an hour or less, and in many cases even just 15 minutes or less (these are usually depicted as screening tests rather than full-blown cognitive assessment tests).

Some decry that only requiring a few minutes to take a cognitive test is rife with problems and seems like a fast-food kind of approach to tackling a very complex topic of measuring someone's cognition.

Those in this camp shudder when these quickie tests are used by people that then go around touting how well they scored.

The counter-argument is that these short-version cognitive tests are reasonable and amount to using a dipstick to gauge how much gasoline there is in the tank of your car. The viewpoint is that it only takes a little bit of measurement to generally know how someone is mentally faring. Once an overall gauge is taken, you can always do a follow-up with a more in-depth cognitive test.

Given all of the preceding discussion, it might be handy to briefly take a look at a well-known cognitive test that has been around since the mid-1990s and continues to actively be in use today, including having been the test that reportedly President Trump took in 2018 according to news reports.

The Famous MoCA Cognitive Test

That test is the Montreal Cognitive Assessment (MoCA) test.

Some mistakenly get confused by the name of the test and think that it is maybe just a test for Canadians since it refers to Montreal in the naming, but the test is globally utilized and was named for being initially developed by researchers in Montreal, Quebec.

Generally, the MoCA is one-page in size, which is handily succinct for doing this kind of testing, and the person taking the test is given 10 minutes to answer the questions. There is some leeway often allowed in the testing time allotted, and also some latitude related to having the person first become oriented to the test and its instructions.

Nonetheless, the person taking the test should not be provided say double the time or anything of that magnitude. The reason why the test should be taken in a prescribed amount of time is that the aspect of time is considered related to cognitive acuity.

In other words, if the person is given more time than others have previously gotten, presumably they can cognitively devote more mental cycles or effort and might do better on the test accordingly.

A timed test is not just about your cognition per se, but also about how fast you think and whether your thinking processes are as fluid as others that have taken the test.

If it took someone an hour and they got a top score, while someone else got a top score in ten minutes, we would be hard-pressed to compare their results. You might liken this to playing timed chess, whereby the longer you have, the more chess moves you can potentially mentally foresee, which is fine in some circumstances, but when trying to make for a balanced playing field, you put a timer on how long each player has to make their move.

That being said, the time allotted for a given test should not be so short as to shortchange the cognitive opportunities, which would once again presumably hamper the measurement of cognition. A chess player that has to say just two seconds to make a move will likely randomly take a shot rather than try to devote mental energy to the task.

In theory, the amount of time provided should be the classic Goldilocks amount, just enough time to allow for a sufficient dollop of mental effort, and not so much time that it inadvertently extends the cognition and perhaps enables a lesser cognitive capacity to use time as a crutch to imbue itself (assuming that's not what the test is attempting to measure).

I am about to explain specific details of the MoCA cognitive test, so if you want to someday take the test, please know that I am about to spoil your freshness (this is a spoiler alert).

The test attempts to cover a lot of cognitive ground, doing so by providing a variety of cognition tasks, including the use of numbers, the use of words, the use of sentences, the use of the alphabet, the use of visual cognitive capabilities such as interpreting images and composing writing, and so on.

That's worth mentioning because a cognitive test that only covered say counting and involved the addition of numbers would be solely focused on your arithmetic cognition. We know that humans have a fuller range of cognitive abilities. As such, a well-balanced cognitive test tries to hit upon a slew of what are considered cognitive dimensions.

Notably, this can be hard to pack into one short test, and raises some criticisms by those that argue it is dubious to have someone undertake a single question on numbers and a single question on words, and so on, and then attempt to generalize overall about their cognition within each respective entire dimension of cognitive facets.

Let's try out a numbers and arithmetic related question.

Are you ready?

You are to start counting from 100 down to 0 and do so by subtracting 7 each time rather than by one.

Okay, your first answer should be 93, and then your next would be 86, and then 79, and so on.

You cannot use a pencil and paper, nor can you use a calculator. This is supposed to be off the top of your head. Using your fingers or toes is also considered taboo.

How did you do?

Try this next one.

Remember these words: Face, Velvet, Church, Daisy, Red.

I want you to look away from these words and say them aloud, without reading them from the page.

In about five minutes, without looking at the page to refresh your memory, try to once again speak aloud what the words were.

What do those cognitive tests signify?

The counting backward is usually a tough one for most people as they do not normally count in that direction. This forces your mind to slow down and think directly about the numbers and the doing of arithmetics in your head. If I had asked you to count by sevens starting at zero and counting upward, you would likely do so with much greater ease, and the effort would be less cognitively taxing on you.

For the word memorization, this is an assessment of your short-term memory capacity. It is only five words versus if I had asked you to remember ten words or fifty words. Some people will try to memorize the five words by imagining an image in their minds of each word, while others might string together the words into making a short story that will allow them to recall the words.

Either way, this is an attempt to exercise your cognition around several facets, involving short-term memory, the ability to follow and abide by instructions, a semblance of encoding words in your mind, and has other mental leveraging cerebral components.

Some of the questions on these cognitive tests are considered controversial.

In the case of MoCA, there is typically a clock drawing task that some cognitive test experts have heartburn about.

You are asked to draw a clock and indicate the time on the clock as being a stated time such as perhaps 10 minutes past 7. In theory, you would draw a circle or something similar, you would write the numbers of 1 to 12 around the oval to represent each hour, and you would then sketch a short line pointing from the center toward the 7, and a longer mark pointing from the center to the 2 position (since the marks for minutes are normally representative of five minutes each).

Why is this controversial as a cognitive test question?

One concern is that in today's world, we tend to use digital clocks that display numerically the time and are less likely to use the conventional circular-shaped clock to represent time anymore.

If a person taking the cognitive test is unfamiliar with oval clocks, does it seem appropriate that they would lose several "cognition" points for poorly accomplishing this task?

This brings up a larger scope qualm about cognitive tests, namely, how can we separate knowledge versus the act of cognition.

I might not know what a conventional clock is and yet have superb cognitive skills. The test is unfairly ascribing knowledge of something in particular to the act of cognition, and so it is falsely measuring one thing that is not necessarily the facet that is being presumably assessed.

Suppose I asked you a question about baseball, such as please go ahead and name the bases or what the various player positions are called. If perchance you know about baseball, you can answer the question, while otherwise, you are going to fail that question.

Do the baseball question and your corresponding answer offer any reasonable semblance of your cognitive capabilities?

In any case, the MoCa cognitive test is usually scored based on a top score of 30, for which the scale typically used is this:

- Score 26-30: No cognitive impairment detected
- Score 18-25: Mild cognitive impairment
- Score 10-17: Moderate cognitive impairment
- Score 00-09: Severe cognitive impairment

Research studies tend to indicate that people with demonstrative Alzheimer's tend to score around 16, ending up in the moderate cognitive impairment category. Presumably, a person with no noticeable cognitive impairment, at least per this specific cognitive test, would score at 26 or higher.

Is it possible to achieve a score in the top tier, the score of 26 or above (presumably suggesting that one does not possess any cognitive impairment), and yet still nonetheless have some form of cognitive deficiency?

Yes, certainly so, since this kind of cognitive test is merely a tiny snapshot or sliver and does not cover an entire battery or gamut of cognition, plus as mentioned earlier there is the possibility of being a priori familiar with the test and/or actively prepare beforehand for the test which can substantively boost performance.

Is it possible to score in the mild, moderate, or severe categories of cognitive impairment and somehow not truly be suffering from cognitive impairment?

Yes, certainly so, since a person might be overly stressed and anxious in taking the test, thus perform poorly due to the situation at hand, or could find the given set of tasks unrelated to their cognition prowess such as perhaps someone that is otherwise ingeniously inventive and cognitively sharp, but find themselves mentally cowed when doing simple arithmetic or memorizing seemingly nonsense words.

All told, it is best to be cautious in interpreting the results of such cognitive tests (and, once again, reinforces the need for a more holistic approach to cognitive assessments).

AI And Cognitive Tests

Another popular topic in the news and one that is seemingly unrelated to this cognitive testing matter is the emergence of AI (hold that thought, for a moment, we'll get back to it).

You are likely numbed by the multitude of AI systems that seem to keep being developed and released into and affecting our everyday lives, including the rise of facial recognition, the advent of Natural Language Processing (NLP) in the case of AI systems such as Alexa and Siri, etc.

On top of that drumbeat, there are the touted wonders of AI, entailing a lot of (rather wild) speculation about where AI is headed and whether AI will eclipse human intelligence, possibly even deciding to take over our planet and choosing to enslave or wipe out humanity.

Why bring up AI, especially if it presumably has nothing to do with cognitive tests and cognitive testing?

Well, for the simple fact that AI does have to do with cognitive testing, very much so.

The presumed goal for AI is to achieve the equivalent of human intelligence, as might somehow be embodied in a machine. We do not yet know what the machine will be, though likely to consist of computers, but the specification does not dictate what it must be, and thus if you could construct a machine via Lego's and duct tape that exhibited human intelligence, more power to you.

In brief, we want to craft artificial cognitive capabilities, which are the presumed crux of human intelligence.

Logically, since that's what we are attempting to accomplish, it stands to reason that we would expect AI to be able to readily pass a human-focused cognitive test since doing so would illustrate that the AI has arrived at similar cognitive capacities.

I don't want to burst anyone's bubble, but there is no AI today that can do any proper semblance of common-sense reasoning, and we are a long way away from having sentient AI.

Bottom-line: AI today would essentially flunk the MoCA cognitive test and any others of similar complexity too.

Some might try to argue and claim that AI and computers can countdown from 100, and can "memorize" words, and do the other stated tasks, but this is a misleading assertion.

Those are tasks undertaken by an AI system that has been constructed for and contrived to perform those specific tasks, and inarguably is a far cry from "understanding" or "comprehending" the test in a manner akin to human capacities and misleadingly anthropomorphizes the matter (for more details, see my analysis at **this link here**).

There is not yet any kind of truly generalizable AI, which some are now calling Artificial General Intelligence (AGI).

As added clarification, there is a famous test in the AI field known as the Turing Test. No AI of today and nor in the foreseeable near future could pass a fully ranging Turing Test, and in some respects, being able to pass a cognitive test like those of MoCA is a variant of a Turing Test (in an extremely narrow way).

AI Cognition And Self-Driving Cars

Another related topic entails the advent of AI-based true self-driving cars.

We are heading toward the use of self-driving cars that involve AI autonomously driving the vehicle, doing so without any human driver at the wheel.

Some wonder whether the AI of today, lacking any kind of common-sense reasoning and nor any inkling of sentience, will be sufficient for driving cars on our public roadways. Critics argue that we are going to have AI substituting for human drivers and yet the AI is insufficiently robust to do so.

Others insist that the driving task does not require the full range of human cognitive capabilities and thus the AI will do just fine in commanding self-driving cars. Do you believe that the AI driving you to the grocery store needs to be able to first pass a cognitive test and showcase that it can adequately draw a clock and indicate the time of day? For now, all we can say is that time will tell.

CHAPTER 11

LIGHTNING STRIKES AND AI SELF-DRIVING CARS

CHAPTER 11
LIGHTNING STRIKES AND AI SELF-DRIVING CARS

According to the National Weather Service (NWS), the month of July is statistically the peak time of the year for lightning strikes within the United States.

Regrettably, July also averages a fatality every three days in the U.S. by someone getting hit and killed via these merciless electrifying bolts from the sky.

If you have ever driven across the Midwest for a summertime family vacation, the number of times that you seem to see lightning streaks on the horizon is nearly countless. At first, the family members packed into the car or van are excited to witness this quite spectacular showcase of nature's fury. Gradually, upon driving nearer and nearer to where the lightning is concentrated, the enthusiasm shifts into trepidation.

I think that we all intuitively realize the powerful destructive force that these streaks of electrical ferocity offer.

It is a phenomenon magnificent to see, but exceedingly dangerous to touch.

Part of the reason that July is such a lethal month involves the twofer at this time of the year.

One aspect is the increased frequency of lightning, brought about because of prevailing weather conditions during the summer months, and the other facet is that people tend to go outside for leisure activities in these same months.

In short, anyone caught outside while lightning is crackling and blitzing all around you, well, they are playing with fire, one might say.

Some assert that many of these fatalities and injuries from lightning are generally preventable. It turns out that people often realize that a thunderstorm is approaching, hearing from afar the booms, and can see the lightning bolts, but tend to ignore the warnings of prevailing doom or danger. More so, people seem to misjudge the pace at which the weather pattern can shift and assume that they will have plenty of time to scamper away before the lightning descends upon them.

This lack of immediately seeking out a safe place is considered a primary reason for people getting jammed up about lightning.

Another possibility is that people might believe that the odds of getting struck by lightning is extremely remote. Sure, they can hear the thunder and are awestruck by the flashes of lightning, but it just seems unlikely that out of all the places that lightning might decide to strike the ground, why would it be near them.

No one can know how many people managed to avoid lightning that otherwise might have clipped them, and thus we are only left with the statistical counts of the ones that unfortunately were struck.

Of those getting hit by lightning, estimates suggest that 10% are killed and the other 90% end-up with some form of a physical disability that can range from short-lasting to long-lasting.

Oddly, some interpret that last statistic to mean that they have a greater chance of surviving the lightning strike, albeit with injuries, and so they shrug off the matter and resign themselves to a willingness to incur the physical disability if it comes down to that consequence.

Here's a handy personal tip: *Do not go outdoors with anyone having that kind of distorted mindset if you think there's any chance of lightning occurring since they are apt to lead you astray.*

People often figure that our tiny sized bodies are not much of an attractive allure and will be saved by obscurity, in comparison to other nearby taller or more bulky objects.

This is faulty logic.

People figure they can hide under a tall tree, or scoot into their tent, or even hide in a public port-a-potty set up in a wooded area.

None of those approaches are especially helpful and you are not demonstrably lowering your chances of getting a lightning surge into your body. The stated rule of thumb is that there is no place outside that is safe from lightning, and seeking concealment in portable restrooms, or under picnic shelters, or within baseball dugouts, those are all a false sense of security.

What can you do?

You might remember as a child being taught to do the infamous "lightning crouch" that purports to be the wisest way to present yourself in a lightning storm.

For those of you that did not perchance undergo that standard lecture at summer camp, the notion is that you should try to minimize your height by crouching, and you should try to minimize your contact with the ground by being on the balls of your feet.

The logical explanation for this contortionist posture is that a person standing straight up is taller and more amenable to enticing the lightning, and thus crouching reduces that semblance of being tall. You might be tempted to think that by laying down on the ground you would certainly fully minimize the height-related concerns, but this adds a new problem, namely that more of your body surface is in contact with the earth that is going to readily transmit the electrical charges into you.

By perching yourself onto the balls of your feet, this provides less of your body touching the ground, while the crouching action aids in keeping your overall height relatively low.

It is an uncomfortable posture, hard for many to undertake, and by some cannot be sustained for any length of time, though the logic underlying the basis for it is readily understandable.

Believe it or not, the lightning crouch recommendation was somewhat rescinded, nearly a dozen years ago, when authorities including the NWS reported that people were misinterpreting the approach and taking it for granted as a surefire means of avoiding getting hit by lightning. Supposedly, people were no longer quite as rapidly escaping a lightning-related area and instead relying upon their false belief that the crouch was their failsafe option.

The authorities now insist that you should not get yourself into a situation whereby the crouch is needed.

Oh, but that was always the case.

One can understand the reticence by authorities to not provide a potential means of enabling people to mislead themselves, yet there is also the practical reality that once you have gotten yourself into a dire predicament, and of course you should not have, nonetheless the crouch is something that can be still considered, some steadfastly argue.

Under what kinds of circumstances do people most often end-up getting killed by lightning?

By knowing the types of outdoor activities involved, you can either avoid those situations (which seems silly, since it is more about doing them in safe ways) or be watchful and have a practical plan for what to do if lightning appears anywhere in the vicinity.

Here is the Top 10 list and the average percentage of deaths in the given category:

1. Fishing (10%)
2. Beach (6%)
3. Camping (5%)
4. Farming (5%)
5. Biking/Motorcycle/ATV (5%)
6. Boating (4%)
7. Social Gathering (4%)
8. Walking to/from home (4%)
9. Roofing (4%)
10. Construction (3%)

Take a moment to ponder the list (note too that these Top 10 account for about 50% of the deaths).

Fishing was the most frequent activity in which a lightning strike led to fatalities. This seems logically plausible since you might be more likely to be fishing in a relatively open area that has no other nearby protective coverage. Being at the beach might seem similar, though perhaps beachgoers are more likely to be near to a beach house and can retreat into the structure.

In any case, there is one item on the list that seems to catch people by extra surprise, and they would not have expected the listed activity to be found on such a list.

Which one is it?

The item indicating lightning strike deaths while biking, or while being on a motorcycle, or when riding on an ATV (these are all included in the fifth item on the list).

Here's why people tend to be surprised.

Each of those modes of transportation has tires, rubber tires, and for various reasons, there is an overwhelming assumption by the public that rubber-based tires will act as a dampener to prevent the electrical charge of lightning from getting to your body, as though the rubber will absorb the electricity on your behalf.

That's not how it works.

This is likely why people also assume that if you hide inside a car from lightning, and if lightning strikes the car, the tires of the car are what will ultimately save you from the electrical zap.

Generally, this is yet another of the myriad of false presumptions about how lightning works and what the tires provide.

Here's what happens when inside a car and the vehicle gets struck by lightning.

First, the lightning is most likely to strike whatever is the topmost element of the car, typically being the antenna, or if there isn't an antenna than simply the overall rooftop lining will suffice.

Next, the electrical charge passes through the outer metallic shell of the car, and then into the tires, which then passes the charge along to the ground.

The tires are not somehow stopping or defusing the electrical charge, and instead are mainly aiding in shoveling the charge into the earth, partially also making use of the steel belts that are within most tires.

My favorite way to describe this matter is by referring to today's cars as being a type of Faraday cage.

Those of you versed in electromagnetism might be aware of the work by the British scientist Michael Faraday and his famous Faraday cage in the early 1800s. Essentially, he experimented with electricity and realized that you could be housed within a conductive metal shell that would prevent you from getting electrified. If you want to see a dramatic version of this facet, there are plenty of online videos on the Internet that show carefully orchestrated examples of the Faraday cage principles (please do not do this at home!).

In the case of lightning, some like to use the phrase of cloud-to-ground to indicate when lightning directly emits from the sky and then hits the ground, doing so without striking any intermediaries. The phrase of cloud-to-vehicle, or more likely cloud-to-vehicle-to-ground, can be used to emphasize that the lightning passes into an intermediary, the vehicle, and then dissipates into the earth.

The thing is, there is a lot of powerful destructive force that is being funneled along via the intermediary, and there is usually a price to be paid.

An antenna is almost surely going to get fried and no longer be functional.

The electrical system of the vehicle is bound to also get fried, and either be partially usable or entirely wrecked.

Components of the car might become engaged with sparks or flames, and splinter into zillions of potent and life-threatening fragments, along with being scattershot into action as though coming out of the barrel of a shotgun.

Those tires, which thankfully shunted the electricity for you, might melt or otherwise become damaged and unusable.

If you have windows in your car that are lined with defrosting wires, the electrical charges that flow through those conductors can cause the glass to instantly break and shatter, possibly spewing shards and endangering anyone inside or nearby the vehicle.

As a topper, these numerous and nearly instantaneous reactions of the vehicle to the lightning strike can right away start a fire. This can produce even greater damages and threaten those that are perhaps sheltering inside the car, though if the car was their only viable option to try and escape the full unmitigated impacts of the lightning, they made a likely sound choice and need to then quickly ascertain their next step.

That last point is crucial, namely that despite the potential adverse effects upon the car, the odds are that you will live, so in that sense, the car is a reasonable refuge when no other better alternatives are available.

Just make sure that while sitting inside the car that you are not holding onto any interior metallic components that are connected to the shell of the car, since doing so puts you into the limelight of where that electricity is going want to flow.

There are oddball instances of connecting yourself inadvertently to the shell of the car, such as having a computer laptop in your lap, which you've plugged into the car's electrical system. This kind of electrical umbilical cord can enable the lightning bolt to flow from the shell into the electrical cord and then into your laptop, subsequently shocking you.

Presumably, the odds of all that occurring seem slim.

Would you really be using your laptop, sitting inside your car, amidst a lightning storm?

Your best bet usually is to be sitting as safely possible in your car seat, with your hands in your lap, and attempting to minimize your body or appendages touching any potential element that could connect with the shell of the car.

Now that we've covered the car-related aspects of lightning strikes, this brings up an interesting related notion.

We are gradually going to witness the advent of AI-based true self-driving cars.

Here's an intriguing question: *What would an AI-based true self-driving car do during a lightning storm and what should a human passenger be doing?*

Let's unpack the matter and see.

Understanding The Levels Of Self-Driving Cars

As a clarification, true self-driving cars are ones that the AI drives the car entirely on its own and there isn't any human assistance during the driving task.

These driverless vehicles are considered a Level 4 and Level 5, while a car that requires a human driver to co-share the driving effort is usually considered at a Level 2 or Level 3. The cars that co-share the driving task are described as being semi-autonomous, and typically contain a variety of automated add-on's that are referred to as ADAS (Advanced Driver-Assistance Systems).

There is not yet a true self-driving car at Level 5, which we don't yet even know if this will be possible to achieve, and nor how long it will take to get there.

Meanwhile, the Level 4 efforts are gradually trying to get some traction by undergoing very narrow and selective public roadway trials, though there is controversy over whether this testing should be allowed per se (we are all life-or-death guinea pigs in an experiment taking place on our highways and byways, some point out).

For semi-autonomous cars, it is important that the public needs to be forewarned about a disturbing aspect that's been arising lately, namely that despite those human drivers that keep posting videos of themselves falling asleep at the wheel of a Level 2 or Level 3 car, we all need to avoid being misled into believing that the driver can take away their attention from the driving task while driving a semi-autonomous car.

Self-Driving Cars And Lightning

For Level 4 and Level 5 true self-driving vehicles, there won't be a human driver involved in the driving task.

All occupants will be passengers.

The AI is doing the driving.

What will the AI do when encountering lightning?

Before we tackle that question, there is an aspect to consider whether a car ought to be driving amidst a lightning storm.

When you opt to go for a drive, doing so as a human driver, hopefully, you tend to check the prevailing weather conditions in the locale of wherever you are going to drive (I realize not everyone is this diligent). Upon discovering lousy conditions, you might decide to drive elsewhere or postpone your trip.

Thus, the first aspect would be whether the AI is programmed to anticipate facets such as lightning conditions wherever you want the AI to drive you.

Some of the existing self-driving cars do not yet have any kind of pre-check about where you want to go and will obediently drive to any stated destination. The onus is on your shoulders to have ascertained that the place you want to go is essentially viable for driving, rather than having the AI figure this out.

Getting the AI to lookup weather conditions and other factors of the destination and the points along the journey is something that can be somewhat readily programmed. Currently, it is considered an edge or corner case, meaning that it is a low priority in comparison to high priorities such as simply getting the self-driving car to drive safely.

The tougher unsolved matter is what the AI should do about the looked-up conditions.

Suppose the AI has identified that there are reports of severe thunderstorms and lightning in a location that you are wanting to head into. Via the use of Natural Language Processing (NLP), similar to Alexa or Siri, the AI warns you that driving to the destination is dangerous.

Should the AI be able to refuse to drive you there?

Your answer might be that of course, the AI can refuse since it is trying to save your life. On the other hand, you might have demonstrative reasons to proceed.

This is an AI Ethics issue that is among many that have not yet been figured out for self-driving cars, and for which until widespread adoption occurs will likely be hidden from view and remain unresolved.

Okay, assume nonetheless that the lightning has suddenly appeared. While riding inside the self-driving car, you might be anxiously looking out the windows, perhaps seeing the lightning as you get closer and closer to it.

Please note that the AI will not have a similar kind of grasp or comprehension about the situation. There is no semblance of common-sense reasoning and nor any measure of sentience in today's AI. As such, you cannot assume that the AI will detect the lightning and "realize" that there is danger afoot.

The odds are that the AI will merely via its cameras and other sensors be able to detect that there are bright sudden flashes of light.

Unless the roadway is otherwise not passable and for which the AI sensors can detect as such, the odds are that the AI is going to just keep driving.

You would need to tell the AI that it should pull over to the side of the road or take an upcoming exit to get to a safe place to then sit out the lightning storm.

Conclusion

You can use the self-driving car as a type of shelter akin to what you might do with any conventional car.

Since a self-driving car is loaded with lots of additional electronics and specialized sensors, the chances are that if the vehicle is struck with lightning, the AI capabilities for driving are going to be fried and the car is not going anywhere, though at least it sacrificed itself to save your life.

Someday, if AI is allotted human rights, does this imply that the AI can object to being a sitting duck in a lightning storm and no longer be willing to act as a sacrificial lamb for saving the human passengers (see my discussion about AI having human rights, at this **link here**)?

That proposition would seem like a bolt out of the blue.

CHAPTER 12
NEANDERTHAL DNA AND AI SELF-DRIVING CARS

CHAPTER 12
NEANDERTHAL DNA AND AI SELF-DRIVING CARS

Scientists are scouring human DNA to try and see if there might be any predispositions toward COVID-19 vulnerability.

This search for genetic risks is partially fostered by the seemingly mysterious facet that some people appear to be more likely to contract coronavirus or suffer particularly adverse consequences upon an infectious onset, doing so while others around them might be overlooked by COVID-19 or have no demonstrative reactions to the scourge.

Modern-day genetic hunters are using all the tricks of the trade-in conducting DNA analyses to possibly discover a fluke or some standout innate genomic characteristic that might account for the widespread differences in how people react upon COVID-19 exposure.

In a heartwarming sign of human compassion, people have rushed forward as volunteers to be studied by these scientific sleuths, hoping in their modest way to contribute toward a breakthrough by merely allowing their DNA to be collected and inspected.

A recently posted early-stage DNA study that has not yet been subjected to the needed peer review process has made some intriguing assertions that are worth contemplating.

This particular study first points out that: "Early in the pandemic it became clear that advanced age is a major risk factor, as well as male sex and some co-morbidities. These risk factors, however, do not fully explain why some have no or mild symptoms while others become seriously ill." In other words, the obvious kinds of metrics such as age, gender, or other easily gathered parameters are seemingly insufficient to figure out who will get COVID-19 and who will not, along with whether the results will be mild or severe.

Digging deeper, the researchers postulated that there might be a DNA quirk that "entered the human population by gene flow from Neanderthals or Denisovans that occurred some 40,000 to 60,000 years ago."

In a Darwinian process, this specific DNA variation potentially wound itself into substantial parts of the world population and has been continuing along without any noticeable impact, perhaps until now, and at this juncture is being considered as a core weakness for the ill-effects of COVID-19.

As the study points out, if their hunch is ultimately proven to be valid, then "gene flow from Neanderthals has tragic consequences."

Again, please realize that this is just a working theory and not yet been scientifically confirmed.

In a sense, we can be sympathetic toward research efforts that are seeking widely to find possible underlying explanations for coronavirus vulnerability. Given the vastness and horrific impacts of the pandemic, aiming to leave no stones unturned would seem a worthwhile shot, even if only vaguely likely and in some cases turn out, in the end, to be misguided.

You might be wondering that if we did discover that this Neanderthal DNA was a legitimate culprit, what good would it do to know about it anyway?

You aren't going to overnight change up your DNA or do some kind of X-Men morphing to alter your genetic makeup to avert COVID-19.

The good news would be that by knowing that such a DNA linkage existed, the public could potentially undertake DNA tests to ascertain who has the genomic attribute and then ready themselves accordingly.

If you found out the DNA lurks within you, it would make sense to take extraordinary precautions to avoid coming in contact with the deadly virus. Meanwhile, those that did not have the DNA indicator would be able to be less worried, though let's be clear that even those not having it would potentially still be able to get the disease and suffer from it (thus, for clarification, the presence of the DNA would suggest that you are especially vulnerable, while the absence would not imply you are invulnerable).

In short, the incidence of a certain element of DNA might produce any one of these three outcomes:

- Relative Susceptibility
- Neutral
- Relative Imperviousness

Let's briefly discuss those three aspects.

First, the suspected piece of Neanderthal DNA might lend itself toward a person housing the genome to be considered *susceptible* to COVID-19, which is what the researchers of that one study are proposing.

Second, given the slew of DNA components that we all have, the assumption is that some parts of our DNA could be considered *neutral* concerning COVID-19, offering neither heightened nor lessened levels of risk.

Thirdly, there is the possibility that an element of your DNA might provide added protections that would make you generally resistant to COVID-19 (that's not what the Neanderthal study posits, but certainly such a theory could arise, namely that there might be other DNA elements that might help someone to extraordinarily withstand the virus).

It is unlikely any such DNA aspect would make you totally invulnerable and so we'll use the word "impervious" to merely suggest that you might have a stronger constitution as a result of having the DNA, therefore possessing a lessened risk associated with contracting and enduring adverse consequences of coronavirus.

Shifting gears, consider that in this discussion so far, the assumption has been that your DNA entails reactions to a physiological manifestation of a virus.

An added twist involves whether there might be cognitive or psychological consequences that can arise too.

Suppose that some people have a piece of DNA in them that makes them more prone to cognitive issues. This is a matter that has been and continues to be studied as part of the research on dementia and other mental difficulties and disorders that seem to occur in humans.

The point being that our DNA can have an impact in two ways:

- Physiological (upon our bodies)
- Psychological (upon our minds and cognition)

Thus, you could have an inherited DNA from Neanderthals that makes you predisposed to a physically transmitted virus such as COVID-19, or perhaps have a hand-me-down DNA that has a predisposition for mental impairments such as dementia.

Not wanting to seem too solemn, but your DNA can readily be prone to both physiological and psychological manifestations, and we cannot arbitrarily claim that those are mutually exclusive conditions. Overall, you might have DNA that can be imbued with some triggering related to physical entailments and some related to thinking oriented ones.

One other quick point before bringing this all together into a neat and tidy bow, there is the matter of whether we even know that a DNA variation exists and what its predispositions portend.

In this dimension, there are two major possibilities:

- Known predisposition (discovered)
- Unknown predisposition (lurking)

Okay, so you could have DNA that is known to have a predisposition and it makes you susceptible to a physiological outcome (that's the working theory about the Neanderthal DNA element, though, right now, we would fairly have to say that it is an *unknown* predisposition, one that is possibly lurking within some of us, but there is as yet full scientific evidence to appropriately support such an assertion).

I trust that you can envision the various permutations and combinations associated with these variables, allowing you to combine the known-versus-unknown predisposition criteria with the physiological and/or psychological impacts, which then is going to produce any of the considered outcomes of relative susceptibility or be neutral or be impervious to some degree.

Wow, that's a mouthful.

Are you ready for a veritable leftfield did-not-see-that-coming twist?

Some believe that humans might have DNA that lurks within some of us and that is going to be triggered upon the advent of AI.

In essence, perhaps there is a Neanderthal DNA strand that has been hiding inside of some of us, not otherwise having had any reason to be triggered or detected, and that upon AI being achieved, namely Artificial Intelligence that is fully sentient (for more on this aspect see **my discussion here**), those humans will find themselves triggered.

You could liken this to those that might have DNA triggered by the COVID-19 virus.

As an important aside, it is somewhat argumentative whether describing this DNA as a "trigger" is the right wording, some would say, and the DNA doesn't need to cause something to happen, while instead, the DNA is pacifically allowing something to happen. Anyway, for the sake of simplicity, let's go ahead and use the word "trigger" but keep in mind the nuances of the semantics involved.

Okay, so we have this working theory that upon achieving AI, which some believe will occur in a moment that is referred to as the singularity (see my explanation at **this link here**), certain people in society will be triggered accordingly due to their DNA.

Absurd, some exhort.

Plain nutty or pure hogwash is another oft-uttered response.

Others point out that it is a reasonable proposition and worthy of rapt attention.

How so?

Well, we have already seemingly agreed that your DNA might have unknown predispositions.

That seems imminently logical.

And we ostensibly agreed that the DNA can enable either or both of physiological or psychological impacts.

This too seems sensible.

The resulting outcome can be that the DNA tends toward susceptibility, or might be neutral, or might be impervious to whatever the triggering mechanism might be.

Thus, there might be a portion of today's world population that has inherited DNA that we do not yet know anything about and for which upon being exposed to AI would trigger a psychological response and be one of susceptibility.

All right, if so, what would that foreshadow?

For those of you that are worried about AI being a potentially existential threat, a notable qualm voiced urgently by for example Elon Musk (see my analysis of his oft vocally stated belief at **the link here**), it could mean that the advent of a fully manifested AI would grab hold of that segment of humanity.

Those with the susceptible DNA might become mental zombies as controlled by AI, doing the bidding of AI, or at least be more inclined toward wanting to appease the AI.

Since the zombie notion seems especially farfetched and causes many to immediately reject the overarching hypothesis, we can stick with the idea that among mankind and when the AI moment comes, there might be some people that will be more willing to accede to AI and less likely to want to resist or repel AI.

Some liken those people to the infamous Borg of the *Star Trek* series (a sci-fi portrayal of living entities that become part of a collective).

Among the entire world population, and at the time that this presumed singularity occurs, there will be apparently some humans that are wary of the AI and will seek to stop or overcome it, and some that will be neutral about the matter, while others will willingly and openly embrace it.

The theory is that this predisposition could be possibly be apriori ascertained to a great extent by our DNA.

You might find this notion implausible and argue that people will choose independently and without regard to their underlying DNA as to whether they will be in favor of or disfavor of the grand appearance of AI.

Perhaps DNA has absolutely nothing to do with it.

On the other hand, it seems impossible to disprove that DNA does not have anything to do with it.

That's a bit of a conundrum in that if you cannot disprove the DNA involvement, you are left with trying to prove the DNA involvement, otherwise, the whole matter is just pure conjecture.

At this time, there doesn't seem to be anyone seriously doing DNA studies to determine this possibility of an AI-triggering hypothesis, and we probably should be happy that no one is since the need to deal with more concrete and near-term issues such as DNA and COVID-19 rightfully ought to be our higher priority today.

Of course, for those that do perceive AI as this looming and worldwide life-threatening extinction existential threat, they might argue that while having a devoted focus on the near-term is quite important, neglecting a further look ahead to the future is shortsighted.

It is indubitably the classic argument that you might win the battle, but ultimately end up losing the war.

Darn, if wishes could come true, it certainly would be handy to have means to study or experiment with this colossal AI triggering theory.

Wait for a second, maybe there is.

Here's an interesting proposition: *Does the advent of AI-based true self-driving cars offer a microcosm scenario for exploring the AI triggering theories?*

Let's unpack the matter and see.

Understanding The Levels Of Self-Driving Cars

As a clarification, true self-driving cars are ones that the AI drives the car entirely on its own and there isn't any human assistance during the driving task.

These driverless vehicles are considered a Level 4 and Level 5, while a car that requires a human driver to co-share the driving effort is usually considered at a Level 2 or Level 3. The cars that co-share the driving task are described as being semi-autonomous, and typically contain a variety of automated add-on's that are referred to as ADAS (Advanced Driver-Assistance Systems).

There is not yet a true self-driving car at Level 5, which we don't yet even know if this will be possible to achieve, and nor how long it will take to get there.

Meanwhile, the Level 4 efforts are gradually trying to get some traction by undergoing very narrow and selective public roadway trials, though there is controversy over whether this testing should be allowed per se (we are all life-or-death guinea pigs in an experiment taking place on our highways and byways, some point out).

Since semi-autonomous cars require a human driver, the adoption of those types of cars won't be markedly different than driving conventional vehicles, so there's not much new per se to cover about them on this topic (though, as you'll see in a moment, the points next made are generally applicable).

For semi-autonomous cars, it is important that the public needs to be forewarned about a disturbing aspect that's been arising lately, namely that despite those human drivers that keep posting videos of themselves falling asleep at the wheel of a Level 2 or Level 3 car, we all need to avoid being misled into believing that the driver can take away their attention from the driving task while driving a semi-autonomous car.

You are the responsible party for the driving actions of the vehicle, regardless of how much automation might be tossed into a Level 2 or Level 3.

Self-Driving Cars And AI Trigger

For Level 4 and Level 5 true self-driving vehicles, there won't be a human driver involved in the driving task.

All occupants will be passengers.

The AI is doing the driving.

One open question about AI self-driving cars is whether the AI must be sentient and have reached the vaunted singularity for true self-driving cars to be possible.

If you believe that sentience must first occur, I can tell you right now that you ought to not be holding your breath for the emergence of true self-driving cars.

I say this because we are nowhere near to achieving that kind of AI, often nowadays referred to as Artificial General Intelligence (AGI).

Today, we do not have any semblance of AGI, such as there is a woeful lack of common-sense reasoning in AI, a crucial element that humans clearly have (when I make this point, some chuckle right away and remark that they doubt many around them have common-sense, but put aside that smarmy view and I believe we can all agree that there is something practically known as common-sense).

Okay, if we are a far cry from AGI, does this imply that we are dead in the water when it comes to having AI self-driving cars?

Not necessarily.

Here's why.

Keep in mind that Level 4 self-driving cars are considered a limited version of self-driving, and rely upon what is called Operational Design Domains (ODD) as a scoping mechanism for their capabilities. In brief, an automaker or self-driving tech firm can declare that their self-driving car and its associated AI will only work in certain conditions or a defined ODD, such as within a specifically pre-mapped downtown area, during the daytime, and not when it is raining or snowing out.

This establishment of drivable boundaries is a helpful way to constrain the dynamics of the driving environment and too can keep the AI from becoming overly complicated to put together.

As such, some would claim that Level 5 might be the arena that requires something akin to AGI, while Level 4 perhaps does not. Essentially, Level 5 is the set of all ODDs, though this is not quite fully apt since you need to know that there are set aside exclusions in the standard itself (such as off-road driving is not included within the scope of the standard).

It would seem plausible that with AI as we roughly know how to construct it today, we should be able to get Level 4 in narrowly determined ODDs to function safely and with an acceptable semblance of risk to society.

Returning to the earlier discussion about DNA and triggering via AI, it would seem highly unlikely that the revered or perhaps feared AGI is in the cards anytime soon, and therefore seemingly there are no viable means to do any initial testing on the matter.

Well, if you are willing to consider Level 4 self-driving cars as a forerunner of AGI, and since the Level 4 via limited ODDs seems reasonably viable in the near-term to mid-term, we might be able to use self-driving cars as a barometer after all.

In short, a proposed assertion is that the adoption of AI-based true self-driving cars of the Level 4 variety will be a means to judge whether people will possibly be triggered by AI, mildly so in the case of Level 4, but serving as a harbinger of what might come further down the pike with AGI.

Even if you do not buy into the DNA as a covert mechanism, perhaps it is reasonable to concede that at least the Level 4 will be the canary in the cage of gauging overall acceptance about AI in general.

Conclusion

You wake up one morning and see some self-driving cars cruising around your neighborhood.

This is wonderful and you smile from ear to ear, pleased to see them.

Is your reaction due to logically and rationally having arrived at such a conclusion, or might a lurking part of your Neanderthal descendant DNA be triggering you to gladly accept the AI and be impulsively spurring you to gleefully welcome these new AI-based intruders?

It could be that you are susceptible to the psychological trigger based on an as-yet-unknown and shadowy part of your inherited DNA.

There is the other side of that coin, namely you might have DNA that causes you to curse those AI self-driving cars and spark you to go out and see if you can stop them.

Lest this seems entirely fanciful, here's a quick bone to chew on.

Could the current polarization in society simply by chance alone, or might we be divided by inherited Neanderthal DNA that has been triggered in recent times?

Let's hope that we can find a means to overcome the polarization, else we might become an extinct species and then, down the road, perhaps some surviving all-knowing AI might look back one day and snicker that we were ultimately and unknowingly doomed by our DNA..

CHAPTER 13
PLANE LANDS ON HIGHWAY AND AI SELF-DRIVING CARS

CHAPTER 12
PLANE LANDS ON HIGHWAY AND AI SELF-DRIVING CARS

Watch out, is it a bird, is it a plane, or is it superman?

Turns out, it was a plane.

A news report and an accompanying video clip recently showcased the harrowing escapade of a small airplane that made an emergency landing on a busy highway, doing so amid everyday car traffic.

As though we all were a fly on the wall, it is fortuitous that a video of the event was captured by the dashcam of a car that was just under the shadow of the plane. The plane went closely overhead and then subsequently touched down onto the lanes ahead of the car.

Thankfully, no one was hurt, and the plane managed to safely enter smackdab into a slew of traffic, ultimately making its way off to the right side of the highway and thus allowing the flowing cars to proceed relatively unabated.

Just another day of dreary car driving and navigating snarls of commuter traffic and, yawn, a plane scooting along on the highway too.

Say what?

Imagine the stories you could tell your co-workers at the office or that you could proffer in a tavern that night over some stiff drinks amid relating tales of what you did that day.

I think it is safe to say that those car drivers had not anticipated when they got up that morning that later in the day they would be getting a front-row seat of watching a plane land on their local highway.

One wonders too, for those cars that were ahead of the landing plane, did the driver's perchance glance at their rearview mirrors and doubt what they are seeing, perhaps questioning their sense of reality and having to do a doubletake?

This does bring up a bit of curiosity about what you might do as a driver that is involuntarily immersed in this kind of situation.

For those that perchance noticed the plane landing behind them, did they push the accelerator pedal to the floor, wanting to avoid getting run down by the fast-moving plane, or did they stay their course and just hope that the pilot was astute enough to be able to keep from overtaking the cars?

It seems doubtful that you would have sufficient time to try and take an offramp to escape the plane. Likewise, slowing down would not seem especially wise, since that might confound the pilot during the effort to gauge where to put down and at what speed to do so.

In the video of this specific instance, the cars that were overshadowed were seemingly able to adjust their speeds, allowing a buffer zone to appear ahead of them, presenting a gap in traffic between the cars behind the plane and the cars ahead of the plane.

Do not though be misled into thinking that the car drivers somehow all collaborated in real-time about how to handle the situation. It appears to be an instinctive maneuver that was independently made by each driver, separately, and that for which collectively had the net effect of aiding the plane to land.

Whether the drivers were intent on helping the plane or maybe instead focused on self-preservation is hard to discern, but the result turned out to be the same either way.

Perhaps the most telling aspect about the mindset of the car drivers was what happened once the plane was on the roadway and had become a ground-based creature rather than one that flies in the air.

The cars tried to squeeze past the plane that was now nothing more than a rather wide and unwelcomed "car" on the highway.

You might be thinking that the cars should come to a complete halt and allow the plane to do the same, or that maybe the cars would stick together as a traffic blockade to prevent other upcoming cars to come suddenly upon the ground cruising plane.

Nope, it was the usual dog-eat-dog world of car driving.

Get out of the way, you miserable plane, I have to get to work on time, or so that seemed to be the viewpoint of the moment.

From time-to-time, throughout the globe, there are similar instances of planes that have landed on a long stretch of road, whether it might be a highway, a freeway, or any street wide enough and lengthy enough to accommodate a plane that needs a temporary and urgent landing strip.

Admittedly, it is a rare event.

When you were doing your driver training as a teenager, it is unlikely that the instructor ever warned you about low flying planes that might land in your path on the roadway ahead. The odds of such an event are so astronomically low that it does not seem worthy of prior attention.

One supposes too that there is not much-specialized practice or extraordinary awareness you need to cope with a landing plane.

Essentially, the plane becomes like an oversized truck and you likely already are versed in dealing with an assortment of unusual vehicles if you have driven for any number of years on a variety of roadways and in assorted traffic conditions.

There is though the shock factor to deal with.

A large-sized truck is going to be readily seen beforehand and you have some reasonable amount of time to prepare for what you might do. In the case of a plane, it miraculously appears out of nowhere, descending from above, and undoubtedly with little warning.

If you are blaring music within your car, you might not hear the telltale sound of a sputtering engine of the plane, nor hear other clueful sounds from above that could give you a hint about what is taking place.

You might perchance have a sunroof open and glance upward to see the plane, though preferably your eyes are normally riveted on the roadway ahead of you and you are not often looking skyward at the clouds and birds flying overhead.

So, the suddenness and out-of-the-blue phenomena are significant factors to be considered in this matter.

Another big question is the nature of what other nearby drivers are going to do.

I would not have much faith in my fellow drivers to remain cool and calm.

Given that many drivers seem to go into road rages or otherwise lose their minds on simple things like when a pick-up truck inadvertently loses an empty can that topples from the back bed, it seems that a lot of drivers are certainly going to have severe angst about a landing plane.

Let's ponder that aspect for a moment.

A key concern would be whether the cars to the left and right or those ahead of or behind you, were going to adjust safely and with proper decorum upon the appearance of the plane. One rightfully would be as worried if not more so that a nearby car driver is going to start a crash or instigate a cascading series of car smashes, doing so as a result of being startled by the plane, rather than the plane doing something untoward per se.

In that context, it might be the case that worrying about the plane is not as paramount as worrying about the rest of the car traffic and what the nearby and potentially zany drivers might do in reaction to this proverbial rabbit-out-of-a-hat appearance of the plane.

There is more to consider too.

Most highways have road signs, often protruding out into the lanes, though stationed on poles and usually high enough to not bother any normal vehicular traffic.

A plane might be overly tall and extra-wide enough to strike those road signs.

That would be bad.

The plane might then do cartwheels or cause significant debris to go flying across the highway, all of which is going to shift the situation into a potentially downright dire and life-threatening circumstance (which, it already is, one would reasonably assume).

The plane could unexpectedly ram a car, or a car could swerve and run into the plane. This might be done directly or be accomplished by an unintentional sideswiping motion and cause a bumping among those vehicles now crowding onto the highway.

When contemplating all the possibilities of how this kind of act can go wrong, it is somewhat surprising to think that anytime a plane makes such a landing that it is not an utter calamity, one that would produce rather sour results for all concerned.

Well, we know that human drivers would undoubtedly be caught off-guard. And, we know too that somehow, by a miracle, when these events occur, it seems that there are usually few if any deaths or injuries.

Pat humanity on the back for contending with such an extraordinary occurrence.

Here's an intriguing question: *With the advent of AI-based true self-driving cars, how would the AI driving system fare if a plane suddenly made an emergency landing on the roadway amidst vehicular traffic?*

Let's unpack the matter and see.

Understanding The Levels Of Self-Driving Cars

As a clarification, true self-driving cars are ones that the AI drives the car entirely on its own and there isn't any human assistance during the driving task.

These driverless vehicles are considered a Level 4 and Level 5, while a car that requires a human driver to co-share the driving effort is usually considered at a Level 2 or Level 3. The cars that co-share the driving task are described as being semi-autonomous, and typically contain a variety of automated add-on's that are referred to as ADAS (Advanced Driver-Assistance Systems).

There is not yet a true self-driving car at Level 5, which we don't yet even know if this will be possible to achieve, and nor how long it will take to get there.

Meanwhile, the Level 4 efforts are gradually trying to get some traction by undergoing very narrow and selective public roadway trials, though there is controversy over whether this testing should be allowed per se (we are all life-or-death guinea pigs in an experiment taking place on our highways and byways, some point out).

Since semi-autonomous cars require a human driver, the adoption of those types of cars won't be markedly different than driving conventional vehicles, so there's not much new per se to cover about them on this topic (though, as you'll see in a moment, the points next made are generally applicable).

For semi-autonomous cars, it is important that the public needs to be forewarned about a disturbing aspect that's been arising lately, namely that despite those human drivers that keep posting videos of themselves falling asleep at the wheel of a Level 2 or Level 3 car, we all need to avoid being misled into believing that the driver can take away their attention from the driving task while driving a semi-autonomous car.

You are the responsible party for the driving actions of the vehicle, regardless of how much automation might be tossed into a Level 2 or Level 3.

Self-Driving Cars And Planes Afoot

For Level 4 and Level 5 true self-driving vehicles, there won't be a human driver involved in the driving task.

All occupants will be passengers.

The AI is doing the driving.

Would the AI be specially trained for a plane landing on the roadway?

Generally, the answer is no.

Right now, the teams that are crafting AI self-driving cars have their hands full with getting the AI to recognize and deal with the day-to-day normalcy of driving a car. The goal currently involves getting a self-driving car to take someone to the grocery store or to work, doing so without blundering into any car accidents, or having anything otherwise go awry (for more about the risks of self-driving cars, see my analysis at **this link here**).

The idea of dealing with a landing plane would be in the so-called edge or corner cases that might, later on, be dealt with by the AI developers. An edge or corner case is placed on a low priority list and sits quietly there, awaiting a day when the needed time and attention might be available to tackle the matter.

I believe that we can all likely agree that it would logical to place the use case of a landing plane to be relatively submerged on the list, rating it as an indubitably less important AI driving task to devised.

Of course, it is easy to make such a statement, though if you someday are riding inside a self-driving car, while on the freeway, and a plane opts to land, you are bound to shake a fist toward the edge cases list and be chagrined that the low-ranked item hadn't yet been implemented.

This brings up the question of whether the "normal" driving by the AI system would be sufficient to cope with the plane landing scenario.

Well, partially yes, and partially no.

It is conceivable that the AI via its sensors such as the cameras, radar, LIDAR, and the other sensory devices would be able to detect the presence of the plane.

For most AI driving systems, an internal virtual computer-based model is being kept at all times about the environment that surrounds the self-driving car. This computational model is populated as a result of the sensor detections that have identified where nearby cars are, and where pedestrians are, and where traffic signs are, etc.

Those sensors are not especially tuned to look upward and thus they are unlikely to spot the plane before it gets low enough to the ground that it begins to seem like a vehicle on the roadway.

Even once the plane lands on the roadway and continues to taxi along, the profile of the plane is unlikely to be something that the AI is trained to recognize.

Generally, via the use of Machine Learning (ML) and Deep Learning (DL), the AI can computationally "recognize" the shapes and sizes of everyday objects such as other cars, trucks, and the like, having been fed thousands upon thousands of prior images for training purposes. As already suggested, there would be little cause currently for the ML/DL to be trained on recognizing a plane, since the onset of a plane into everyday traffic is a slim odds act.

In short, the AI might not be able to pattern recognize what the new object is. The oddball shape and the weird pings and visual appearance is likely to stymy the AI in terms of what the object is and what it might do.

Nonetheless, the AI will hopefully ascertain that there is an object ahead, the object is moving, the object is quite obtrusive, and thus the AI will resort to being cautious in approaching the unknown thing.

Meanwhile, as I also mentioned earlier, the other matter to be coped with is the reaction of other cars that are nearby.

Human drivers that are driving in their cars are bound to take sudden actions, for which the AI is relatively better prepared to cope with than dealing with the plane itself.

The AI might not be able to "deduce" why those cars and their drivers are reacting, but at least the AI is usually set up to deal with circumstances of human-driven cars that go haywire such as if they were all trying to avoid a dropped ladder onto the roadway or someone suddenly got a flat tire.

If there are other AI self-driving cars involved in this plane landing, those self-driving cars are trying to react too to whatever the other human-driven cars are doing.

Keep in mind that not all AI driving systems are the same, namely that each of the automakers or self-driving tech firms are tending to develop their proprietary versions. This means that each of the AI driving systems per brand of the self-driving car will likely have its way of dealing with traffic, thus, not all of the self-driving cars will necessarily be reacting to the scene in the same way.

One potential added plus for the self-driving cars is that they are likely to be equipped with V2V (vehicle-to-vehicle) electronic communication.

The V2V allows the AI of the self-driving cars to each message the other about the roadway status. This can be used to forewarn each other about traffic blockages and aspects such as debris that a self-driving car has detected, sending along a message to other self-driving cars to let them know beforehand that there is something to be avoided.

It is quite unlikely that the V2V would have any provision for conferring about a landing plane, though at least the V2V might be used to warn about an unknown object and also alert about the driving reactions of the human-driven cars.

Does it matter that the AI would not "know" or "comprehend" that the situation involved a landing plane?

There is no doubt that the AI would likely be better off in this situation if it had been crafted to include a plane landing scenario. But let's be abundantly clear, even if the AI had been coded and prepared for this obscure use case, it would still not "understand" what is going on.

Despite whatever the mass media might seem to claim, there is not any AI that is yet able to have any semblance of common-sense or sentience of reasoning.

Such AI does not exist today.

There is a desired goal of someday arriving at Artificial General Intelligence (AGI), which would encompass the full gamut of human intelligence. That day, including the vaunted notion of a singularity that presumably will be when we have AI suddenly switch over into sentience, does not seem anywhere on the horizon (see my discussion at **this link here**).

The point overall herein is that for the plane landing scenario, the AI would not "comprehend" what is happening, no matter whether the AI developers had coded for the AI to be so prepared, and would still only handle the matter in a limited way, unlike a human driver that would presumably have a deeper semblance of what is taking place.

One counterargument is that though the AI would not grasp the nature of the moment, nor would it be prone to an emotional reaction, which human drivers might do, and nor would the AI be distracted or drunk, any of which a human driver might embody.

Conclusion

Now that I've discussed the landing of a plane on a traffic-ridden highway, do you feel mentally prepared for the possibility of such a circumstance someday befalling you?

The odds of it occurring are quite remote, and when it happens the dynamics of the moment will ascertain to a great extent whether the outcome is a positive one or a potentially adverse one.

An AI self-driving car would do what it does, making use of its customary driving capacities, and hopefully, that would be sufficient to keep from getting into a wreck, though there is no guarantee and similarly no such guarantee for a human-driven car either.

I am decidedly not advocating that you continually look up at the skies while you are behind the wheel of a car since I'd much rather that you keep your focus on the road directly ahead of you, and not be searching endlessly and fruitlessly for a plane that is going to land in your lane.

Of course, we might all eventually have flying cars anyway, and thus looking upward will be a normal part of passing your driver's license certification test.

.

CHAPTER 14
TURING TEST AND AI SELF-DRIVING CARS

CHAPTER 14
TURING TEST
AND
AI SELF-DRIVING CARS

How will we know when the world has arrived at AI?

To clarify, there are lots of claims these days about computers that embody AI, implying that the machine is the equivalent of human intelligence, but you need to be wary of those rather brash and outright disingenuous assertions.

The goal of those that develop AI consists of one day being able to have a computer-based system that can exhibit human intelligence, doing so in the widest and deepest of ways that human intelligence exists and showcases itself.

There is not any such AI as yet devised.

The confusion over this matter has gotten so out-of-hand that the field of AI has been forced into coming up with a new moniker to express the outsized revered goal of AI, proclaiming now that the goal is to arrive at Artificial General Intelligence (AGI).

This is being done in hopes of emphasizing to laymen and the public-at-large that the vaunted and desired AI would include common-sense reasoning and a slew of other intelligence-like capacities that humans have (for details about the notion of Strong AI versus Weak AI, along with Narrow AI too).

Since there is quite some muddling going on about what constitutes AI and what does not, you might wonder how we will ultimately be able to ascertain whether AI has been unequivocally attained.

We rightfully should insist on having something more than a mere provocateur proclamation and we ought to remain skeptical about anyone that holds forth an AI system that they declare is the real deal.

Looks alone would be insufficient to attest to the arrival.

There are plenty of parlor stunts in the AI bag-of-tricks that can readily fool many into believing that they are witnessing an AI of amazing human-like qualities.

No, just taking someone's word for AI having been accomplished or simply kicking the tires of the AI to feebly gauge its merits is insufficient and inarguably will not do.

There must be a better way.

Those within the AI field have tended to consider a type of test known as the Turing Test to be the gold standard for seeking to certify AI as being the venerated AI or semantically the AGI.

As named after its author, Alan Turing, the well-known mathematician and early pioneer in the computer sciences, the Turing Test was devised in 1950 and remains pertinent still today. Parsimoniously, the Turing Test is relatively easy to describe and indubitably straightforward to envision.

Here's a quick rundown about the nature of the Turing Test.

Imagine that we had a human hidden behind a curtain, and a computer hidden behind a second curtain, such that you could not by sight alone discern what or who is residing behind the two curtains.

The human and the computer are considered contestants in a contest that will be used to try and figure out whether AI has been reached.

Some prefer to call them "subjects" rather than contestants, due to the notion that this is perhaps more of an experiment than it is a game show, but the point is that they are "participants" in a form of challenge or contest involving wits and intelligence.

No arm wrestling is involved, and nor any other physical acts.

The testing process is entirely about intellectual acumen.

A moderator serves as an interrogator (also referred to as a "judge" because of the designated deciding role in this matter) and proceeds to ask questions of the two participants that are hidden behind the curtains.

Based on the answers provided to the questions, the moderator will attempt to indicate which curtain hides the human and which curtain hides the computer. This is a crucial judging aspect. Simply stated, if the moderator is unable to distinguish between the two contestants as to which is the human and which is the computer, presumably the computer has sufficiently "proven" that it is the equivalent of human intelligence.

Turing originally coined this the "imitation game" since it involves the AI trying to imitate the intelligence of humans. Note that the AI does not necessarily have to be crafted in the same manner as humans, and thus there is no requirement that the AI has a brain or uses neurons and such. Thus, those devising AI are welcome to use Lego's and duct tape if that will do the job to achieve the equivalence of human intelligence.

To successfully pass the Turing Test, the computer embodying AI will have had to answer the posed questions with the same semblance of intelligence as a human. An unsuccessful passing of the Turing Test would occur if the moderator was able to announce which curtain housed the computer, thus implying that there was some kind of telltale clue that gave away the AI.

Overall, this seems to be a rather helpful and effective way to ferret out AI that is the aspirational AGI versus AI that is something less so.

Of course, like most things in life, there are some potential gotchas and twists to this matter.

Imagine we have set up a stage with two curtains and a podium for the moderator. The contestants are completely hidden from view.

The moderator steps up to the podium and asks one of the contestants how to make a bean burrito, and then asks the other contestant how to make a bologna sandwich. Let's assume that the answers are apt and properly describe the effort involved in making a bean burrito and in making a bologna sandwich, respectively so.

The moderator decides to stop asking any further questions.

Voila, the moderator announces, the AI is indistinguishable from human intelligence and therefore this AI is declared forthwith as having reached the pinnacle of AI, the long sought after AGI.

Should we accept this decree?

I don't think so.

This highlights an important element of the Turing Test, namely that the moderator needs to ask a sufficient range and depth of questions that will help root out the embodiment of intelligence. When the questions are shallow or insufficient, any conclusion reached is spurious at best.

Please know too that there is not a specified set of questions that have been vetted and agreed upon as the "right" ones to be asked during a Turing Test. Sure, some researchers have tried to propose the types of questions that ought to be asked, but this is an ongoing debate and to some extent illuminates that we are still not even quite sure of what intelligence per se consists of (it is hard to identify metrics and measures for that which is relatively ill-defined and ontologically squishy).

Another issue exists about the contestants and their behavior.

For example, suppose the moderator asks each of the contestants whether they are human.

The human can presumably answer yes, doing so honestly. The AI could say that it is not a human, opting to be honest, but then this decidedly ruins the test and seemingly undermines the spirit of the Turing Test.

Perhaps the AI should lie and say that it is the human. There are ethicists though that would decry such a response and argue that we do not want AI to be a liar, therefore no AI should ever be allowed to lie.

Of course, the human might lie, and deny that they are the human in this contest. If we are seeking to make AI that is the equivalent of human intelligence, and if humans lie, which we all know that humans certainly do lie from time-to-time, shouldn't the AI also be allowed to lie?

Anyway, the point is that the contestants can either strive to aid the Turing Test or can try to undermine or distort the Turing Test, which some say is fine, and that it is up the moderator to figure out what to do.

All's fair in love and war, as they say.

How tricky do we want the moderator to be?

Suppose the moderator asks each of the contestants to calculate the answer to a complex mathematical equation. The AI can speedily arrive at a precise answer of 8.27689459, while the human struggles to do the math by hand and come up with an incorrect answer of 9.

Aha, the moderator has fooled the AI into revealing itself, and likewise the human into revealing that they are a human, doing so by asking a question that the computer-based AI readily could answer and that a human would have a difficult time answering.

Believe it or not, for this very reason, AI researchers have proposed the introduction of what some call Artificial Stupidity. The idea is that the AI will purposely attempt to be "stupid" by sharing answers as though they were prepared by a human. In this instance, the AI might report that the answer is 8, thus the response is a lot like the one by the human.

You can imagine that having AI purposely try to make mistakes or falter is not something that everyone necessarily agrees is a good thing.

We do allow for humans to make guffaws, but having AI that does so, especially when it "knows better" would seem like a dangerous and undesirable slippery slope.

The Reverse Turing Test Rears Its Head

I've now described for you the overall semblance of the Turing Test.

Next, let's consider a variation that some like to call a Reverse Turing Test.

Here's how that works.

The human contestant decides they are going to pretend that they are the AI. As such, they will attempt to provide answers that are indistinguishable from the AI's type of answers.

Recall that the AI in the conventional Turing Test is trying to seem indistinguishable from a human. In the Reverse Turing Test, the human contestant is trying to "reverse" the notion and act as though they were the AI and therefore indistinguishable from the AI.

Well, that seems mildly interesting, but why would the human do this?

This might be done for fun, kind of laughs for people that enjoy developing AI systems. It could also be done as a challenge, trying to mimic or imitate an AI system, and betting whether you can do so successfully or not.

Another reason and one that seems to have more chops or merit consists of doing what is known as a Wizard of Oz.

When a programmer is developing software, they will sometimes pretend that they are the program and use a facade front-end or interface to have people interact with the budding system, though those users do not know that the programmer is watching their interaction and ready to interact too (doing so secretively from behind the screen and without revealing their presence).

Doing this type of development can reveal how the end-users are having difficulties using the software, and meanwhile, they remain within the flow of the software by the fact that the programmer intervened, quietly, to overcome any of the computer system deficiencies that might have disrupted the effort.

Perhaps this makes clear why it is often referred to as a Wizard of Oz, involving the human staying in-the-loop and secretly playing the role of Oz.

Getting back to the Reverse Turing Test, the human contestant might be pretending to be the AI to figure out where the AI is lacking, and thus be better able to enhance the AI and continue on the quest toward AGI.

In that manner, a Reverse Turing Test can be used for perhaps both fun and profit.

Turing Test Upside-Down And Right Side Up

Some believe that we might ultimately be headed toward what is sometimes called the Upside-Down Turing Test.

Yes, that's right, this is yet another variant.

In the Upside-Down Turing Test, replace the moderator with AI.

Say what?

This less discussed variant involves having AI be the judge or interrogator, rather than a human doing so. The AI asks questions of the two contestants, still consisting of an AI and a human, and then renders an opinion about which is which.

Your first concern might be that the AI seems to have two seats in this game, and as such, it is either cheating or simply a nonsensical arrangement. Those that postulate this variant are quick to point out that the original Turing Test has a human as a moderator and a human as a contestant, thus, why not allow the AI to do the same.

The instant retort is that humans are different from each other, while AI is presumably the same thing and not differentiable.

That's where those interested in the Upside-Down Turing Test would say you are wrong in that assumption. They contend that we are going to have multitudes of AI, each of which will be its instance, and be akin to how humans are each their instance (AI will be heterogeneous and not homogenous, in a sense).

The counterargument is that the AI is presumably going to be merely some kind of software and a machine, all of which can be readily combined into other software and machines, but that you cannot readily combine humans and their brains.

We each have a brain intact within our skulls, and there are no known means to directly combine them or mesh them with others.

Anyway, this back-and-forth continues, each proffering a rejoinder, and it is not readily apparent that the Upside-Down variant can be readily discarded as a worthwhile possibility.

As you might imagine, there is an Upside-Down Turing Test and also an Upside-Down Reverse Turing Test, mirroring the aspect of the conventional Turing Test and its counterpart the Reverse Turing Test (some, by the way, do not like the use of Upside-Down and instead insist that this added variant is merely another offshoot of the Reverse Turing Test).

You might begrudgingly agree to let the AI be in two places at once, and have one AI as the interrogator and one as a contestant.

What good does that do anyway?

One thought is that it helps to potentially further showcase whether AI is intelligent, which might be evident as to the questioning and the nature of how the AI digests the answers being provided, illustrating the AI's capacity as the equivalent of a human judge or interrogator.

That's the mundane or humdrum explanation.

Are you ready for the scary version?

It has to do with intelligence, as I'll describe next.

Some believe that AI will eventually exceed human intelligence, arriving at Artificial Super Intelligence (ASI).

The word "super" is not meant to imply superman or superwoman kinds of powers, and instead of that, the intelligence of the AI is beyond our human intelligence, though not necessarily able to leap tall buildings or move faster than a speeding bullet.

Nobody can say what this ASI or superintelligence might be able to think of, and perhaps we as humans are so limited in our intelligence that we cannot see beyond our limits. As such, the ASI might be intelligent in ways that we cannot foresee.

That's why some are considering AI or AGI to potentially be an existential threat to humanity (this is something that for example Elon Musk has continued to evoke, see my coverage at **this link here**), and the ASI presumed to be even more so a potential menace.

If you are interested in this existential threat argument, as I've pointed out repeatedly (see **the link here**), there are just as many ways to conjure that the AI or AGI or ASI will help mankind and aid us in flourishing as there are the doomsday scenarios of our being squashed like a bug.

That being said, it certainly makes sense to be prepared for the latter, due to the rather obvious discomfort and a sad result that would accrue down that path (I assume none of what to be quelled like bugs).

Returning to the Upside-Down Turing Test, it could be that an ASI would sit in the moderator's seat and be judging whether "conventional" AI has yet reached the aspirational level of AI that renders it able to pass the Turing Test and be considered indistinguishable from human intelligence.

Depending on how far down the rabbit hole you want to go on this, at some point the Turing Test might have two seats for the ASI, and one seat for AI. This means that the moderator would be an ASI, while there is conventional AI as a contestant and another ASI as the other contestant.

Notice that there is not a human involved at all.

Maybe we ought to call this the Takeover Turing Test.

No humans needed; no humans allowed.

Conclusion

It is unlikely that AI is going to be crafted simply for the sake of making AI, and instead, there will be a purpose-driven rationale for why humans opt to create AI.

One such purpose involves the desire to have self-driving cars.

A true self-driving car is one that has AI driving the car and there is no need for a human driver. The only role of a human would be as a passenger, but not at all as a driver.

A vexing question right now is what level or degree of AI is needed to achieve self-driving cars.

Some believe that until AI has arrived at the aspirational AGI, we will not have true self-driving cars. Indeed, those with such an opinion would likely say that the AI has to achieve sentience, perhaps doing so in a moment of switchover from automation into a spark of being that is called the moment of singularity (for more on this, see my analysis at **this link here**).

Hogwash, some counter, and insist that we can get AI that is not necessarily Turing Test worthy but that can nonetheless safely and properly drive cars.

To be clear, right now there is not any kind of AI self-driving car that approaches anything like AGI, and so for the moment, we are faced with trying to decide if "every day" AI can be sufficient to drive a car.

When you ponder the situation, in one viewpoint, you could say that we are conducting a Turing Test on our streets today, allowing self-driving cars to cruise on our streets amongst human-driven cars, and if the AI-driven car is indistinguishable in terms of driving properly, it is passing a driver-oriented Turing Test.

Critics worry that we are allowing a Turing Test to take place in front of our eyes, potentially endangering the rest of us, involuntarily dragged into a rather dicey experiment, while others argue that with the use of back-up human-drivers in the vehicles we are presumably okay (for more about the qualms of this facet, see **my discussion here**).

In any case, the Turing Test is an important tool in the toolbox of striving toward AI, and whether you are using the traditional Turing Test, the Reverse Turing Test, or the Upside-Down Turing Test, let's aim to create AI that wants to be friends and not be our downfall.

That's probably the most important test of all!

APPENDIX

APPENDIX A
TEACHING WITH THIS MATERIAL

The material in this book can be readily used either as a supplemental to other content for a class, or it can also be used as a core set of textbook material for a specialized class. Classes where this material is most likely used include any classes at the college or university level that want to augment the class by offering thought provoking and educational essays about AI and self-driving cars.

In particular, here are some aspects for class use:

- Computer Science. Studying AI, autonomous vehicles, etc.
- Business. Exploring technology and it adoption for business.
- Sociology. Sociological views on the adoption and advancement of technology.

Specialized classes at the undergraduate and graduate level can also make use of this material.

For each chapter, consider whether you think the chapter provides material relevant to your course topic. There is plenty of opportunity to get the students thinking about the topic and force them to decide whether they agree or disagree with the points offered and positions taken. I would also encourage you to have the students do additional research beyond the chapter material presented (I provide next some suggested assignments they can do).

RESEARCH ASSIGNMENTS ON THESE TOPICS

Your students can find background material on these topics, doing so in various business and technical publications. I list below the top ranked AI related journals. For business publications, I would suggest the usual culprits such as the Harvard Business Review, Forbes, Fortune, WSJ, and the like.

Here are some suggestions of homework or projects that you could assign to students:

a) Assignment for foundational AI research topic: Research and prepare a paper and a presentation on a specific aspect of Deep AI, Machine Learning, ANN, etc. The paper should cite at least 3 reputable sources. Compare and contrast to what has been stated in this book.

b) Assignment for the Self-Driving Car topic: Research and prepare a paper and Self-Driving Cars. Cite at least 3 reputable sources and analyze the characterizations. Compare and contrast to what has been stated in this book.

c) Assignment for a Business topic: Research and prepare a paper and a presentation on businesses and advanced technology. What is hot, and what is not? Cite at least 3 reputable sources. Compare and contrast to the depictions in this book.

d) Assignment to do a Startup: Have the students prepare a paper about how they might startup a business in this realm. They must submit a sound Business Plan for the startup. They could also be asked to present their Business Plan and so should also have a presentation deck to coincide with it.

You can certainly adjust the aforementioned assignments to fit to your particular needs and the class structure. You'll notice that I ask for 3 reputable cited sources for the paper writing based assignments. I usually steer students toward "reputable" publications, since otherwise they will cite some oddball source that has no credentials other than that they happened to write something and post it onto the Internet. You can define "reputable" in whatever way you prefer, for example some faculty think Wikipedia is not reputable while others believe it is reputable and allow students to cite it.

The reason that I usually ask for at least 3 citations is that if the student only does one or two citations they usually settle on whatever they happened to find the fastest. By requiring three citations, it usually seems to force them to look around, explore, and end-up probably finding five or more, and then whittling it down to 3 that they will actually use.

I have not specified the length of their papers, and leave that to you to tell the students what you prefer. For each of those assignments, you could end-up with a short one to two pager, or you could do a dissertation length paper. Base the length on whatever best fits for your class, and the credit amount of the assignment within the context of the other grading metrics you'll be using for the class.

I mention in the assignments that they are to do a paper and prepare a presentation. I usually try to get students to present their work. This is a good practice for what they will do in the business world. Most of the time, they will be required to prepare an analysis and present it. If you don't have the class time or inclination to have the students present, then you can of course cut out the aspect of them putting together a presentation.

If you want to point students toward highly ranked journals in AI, here's a list of the top journals as reported by *various citation counts sources* (this list changes year to year):

- Communications of the ACM
- Artificial Intelligence
- Cognitive Science
- IEEE Transactions on Pattern Analysis and Machine Intelligence
- Foundations and Trends in Machine Learning
- Journal of Memory and Language
- Cognitive Psychology
- Neural Networks
- IEEE Transactions on Neural Networks and Learning Systems
- IEEE Intelligent Systems
- Knowledge-based Systems

GUIDE TO USING THE CHAPTERS

For each of the chapters, I provide next some various ways to use the chapter material. You can assign the tasks as individual homework assignments, or the tasks can be used with team projects for the class. You can easily layout a series of assignments, such as indicating that the students are to do item "a" below for say Chapter 1, then "b" for the next chapter of the book, and so on.

a) What is the main point of the chapter and describe in your own words the significance of the topic,

b) Identify at least two aspects in the chapter that you agree with, and support your concurrence by providing at least one other outside researched item as support; make sure to explain your basis for disagreeing with the aspects,

c) Identify at least two aspects in the chapter that you disagree with, and support your disagreement by providing at least one other outside researched item as support; make sure to explain your basis for disagreeing with the aspects,

d) Find an aspect that was not covered in the chapter, doing so by conducting outside research, and then explain how that aspect ties into the chapter and what significance it brings to the topic,

e) Interview a specialist in industry about the topic of the chapter, collect from them their thoughts and opinions, and readdress the chapter by citing your source and how they compared and contrasted to the material,

f) Interview a relevant academic professor or researcher in a college or university about the topic of the chapter, collect from them their thoughts and opinions, and readdress the chapter by citing your source and how they compared and contrasted to the material,

g) Try to update a chapter by finding out the latest on the topic, and ascertain whether the issue or topic has now been solved or whether it is still being addressed, explain what you come up with.

The above are all ways in which you can get the students of your class involved in considering the material of a given chapter. You could mix things up by having one of those above assignments per each week, covering the chapters over the course of the semester or quarter.

As a reminder, here are the chapters of the book and you can select whichever chapters you find most valued for your particular class:

Companion Book By This Author

Advances in AI and Autonomous Vehicles: Cybernetic Self-Driving Cars

Practical Advances in Artificial Intelligence (AI) and Machine Learning

by

Dr. Lance B. Eliot, MBA, PhD

Chapter Title

This title is available via Amazon and other book sellers

Companion Book By This Author

Self-Driving Cars:
"The Mother of All AI Projects"

by Dr. Lance B. Eliot, MBA, PhD

Chapter Title

This title is available via Amazon and other book seller

Companion Book By This Author

Innovation and Thought Leadership on Self-Driving Driverless Cars

by Dr. Lance B. Eliot, MBA, PhD

Chapter Title

This title is available via Amazon and other book sellers

Companion Book By This Author

New Advances in AI Autonomous Driverless Cars Self-Driving Cars

by Dr. Lance B. Eliot, MBA, PhD

This title is available via Amazon and other book sellers

Companion Book By This Author

Introduction to Driverless Self-Driving Cars

by Dr. Lance B. Eliot, MBA, PhD

Chapter Title

This title is available via Amazon and other book sellers

Companion Book By This Author

Autonomous Vehicle Driverless Self-Driving Cars and Artificial Intelligence

by Dr. Lance B. Eliot, MBA, PhD

Chapter Title

This title is available via Amazon and other book sellers

Companion Book By This Author

Transformative Artificial Intelligence Driverless Self-Driving Cars

by Dr. Lance B. Eliot, MBA, PhD

Chapter Title

This title is available via Amazon and other book sellers

Companion Book By This Author

Disruptive Artificial Intelligence and Driverless Self-Driving Cars

by Dr. Lance B. Eliot, MBA, PhD

Chapter Title

This title is available via Amazon and other book sellers

Companion Book By This Author

State-of-the-Art
AI Driverless Self-Driving Cars

by Dr. Lance B. Eliot, MBA, PhD

Chapter Title

This title is available via Amazon and other book sellers

Companion Book By This Author

Top Trends in AI Self-Driving Cars

by Dr. Lance B. Eliot, MBA, PhD

Chapter Title

This title is available via Amazon and other book sellers

Companion Book By This Author

AI Innovations and Self-Driving Cars

by Dr. Lance B. Eliot, MBA, PhD

Chapter Title

This title is available via Amazon and other book sellers

Companion Book By This Author

Crucial Advances for
AI Self-Driving Cars

by Dr. Lance B. Eliot, MBA, PhD

Chapter Title

This title is available via Amazon and other book sellers

Companion Book By This Author

Sociotechnical Insights and AI Driverless Cars

by Dr. Lance B. Eliot, MBA, PhD

Chapter Title

This title is available via Amazon and other book sellers

Companion Book By This Author

Pioneering Advances for AI Driverless Cars

by Dr. Lance B. Eliot, MBA, PhD

Chapter Title

This title is available via Amazon and other book sellers

Companion Book By This Author

Leading Edge Trends for AI Driverless Cars

by Dr. Lance B. Eliot, MBA, PhD

Chapter Title

This title is available via Amazon and other book sellers

Companion Book By This Author

The Cutting Edge of AI Autonomous Cars

by Dr. Lance B. Eliot, MBA, PhD

Chapter Title

This title is available via Amazon and other book sellers

Companion Book By This Author

The Next Wave of
AI Self-Driving Cars

by Dr. Lance B. Eliot, MBA, PhD

Chapter Title

This title is available via Amazon and other book sellers

Companion Book By This Author

Revolutionary Innovations of AI Self-Driving Cars

by Dr. Lance B. Eliot, MBA, PhD

This title is available via Amazon and other book sellers

Companion Book By This Author

AI Self-Driving Cars
Breakthroughs

by Dr. Lance B. Eliot, MBA, PhD

Chapter Title

This title is available via Amazon and other book sellers

Companion Book By This Author

Trailblazing Trends for
AI Self-Driving Cars

by Dr. Lance B. Eliot, MBA, PhD

Chapter Title

This title is available via Amazon and other book sellers

Companion Book By This Author

Ingenious Strides for
AI Driverless Cars

by Dr. Lance B. Eliot, MBA, PhD

Chapter Title

This title is available via Amazon and other book sellers

Companion Book By This Author

AI Self-Driving Cars Inventiveness

by Dr. Lance B. Eliot, MBA, PhD

Chapter Title

This title is available via Amazon and other book sellers

Companion Book By This Author

Visionary Secrets of
AI Driverless Cars

by Dr. Lance B. Eliot, MBA, PhD

Chapter Title

Companion Book By This Author

Spearheading
AI Self-Driving Cars

by Dr. Lance B. Eliot, MBA, PhD

Chapter Title

1 Eliot Framework for AI Self-Driving Cars

2 Artificial Pain and AI Self-Driving Cars

3 Stop-and-Frisks and AI Self-Driving Cars

4 Cars Careening and AI Self-Driving Cars

5 Sounding Out Car Noises and AI Self-Driving Cars

6 No Speed Limit Autobahn and AI Self-Driving Car

7 Noble Cause Corruption and AI Self-Driving Cars

8 AI Rockstars and AI Self-Driving Cars

This title is available via Amazon and other book sellers

Companion Book By This Author

Spurring AI Self-Driving Cars

by Dr. Lance B. Eliot, MBA, PhD

Chapter Title

This title is available via Amazon and other book sellers

Companion Book By This Author

Avant-Garde
AI Driverless Cars

by Dr. Lance B. Eliot, MBA, PhD

Chapter Title

This title is available via Amazon and other book sellers

Companion Book By This Author

AI Self-Driving Cars Evolvement

by Dr. Lance B. Eliot, MBA, PhD

Chapter Title

This title is available via Amazon and other book sellers

Companion Book By This Author

AI Driverless Cars
Chrysalis

by Dr. Lance B. Eliot, MBA, PhD

Chapter Title

This title is available via Amazon and other book sellers

Companion Book By This Author

AI Self-Driving Cars Trendsetting

by Dr. Lance B. Eliot, MBA, PhD

Chapter Title

This title is available via Amazon and other book sellers

Companion Book By This Author

AI Autonomous Cars Forefront

by Dr. Lance B. Eliot, MBA, PhD

Chapter Title

This title is available via Amazon and other book sellers

Companion Book By This Author

AI Autonomous Cars Emergence

by Dr. Lance B. Eliot, MBA, PhD

Chapter Title

This title is available via Amazon and other book sellers

Companion Book By This Author

AI Autonomous Cars Progress

by Dr. Lance B. Eliot, MBA, PhD

Chapter Title

This title is available via Amazon and other book sellers

Companion Book By This Author

AI Self-Driving Cars Prognosis

by Dr. Lance B. Eliot, MBA, PhD

This title is available via Amazon and other book sellers

Companion Book By This Author

AI Self-Driving Cars
Momentum

by Dr. Lance B. Eliot, MBA, PhD

Chapter Title

This title is available via Amazon and other book sellers

Companion Book By This Author

AI Self-Driving Cars
Headway

by Dr. Lance B. Eliot, MBA, PhD

Chapter Title

This title is available via Amazon and other book sellers

Companion Book By This Author

AI Self-Driving Cars Autonomy

by Dr. Lance B. Eliot, MBA, PhD

Chapter Title

This title is available via Amazon and other book sellers

Companion Book By This Author

AI Driverless Cars Transmutation

by Dr. Lance B. Eliot, MBA, PhD

Chapter Title

This title is available via Amazon and other book sellers

Companion Book By This Author

AI Driverless Cars Potentiality

by Dr. Lance B. Eliot, MBA, PhD

Chapter Title

This title is available via Amazon and other book sellers

Companion Book By This Author

AI Driverless Cars
Realities

by Dr. Lance B. Eliot, MBA, PhD

Chapter Title

This title is available via Amazon and other book sellers

Companion Book By This Author

AI Self-Driving Cars
Materiality

by Dr. Lance B. Eliot, MBA, PhD

Chapter Title

This title is available via Amazon and other book sellers

Companion Book By This Author

AI Self-Driving Cars
Accordance

by Dr. Lance B. Eliot, MBA, PhD

Chapter Title

This title is available via Amazon and other book sellers

Companion Book By This Author

AI Self-Driving Cars
Equanimity

by Dr. Lance B. Eliot, MBA, PhD

Chapter Title

This title is available via Amazon and other book sellers

Companion Book By This Author

AI Self-Driving Cars
Divulgement

by Dr. Lance B. Eliot, MBA, PhD

Chapter Title

This title is available via Amazon and other book sellers

Companion Book By This Author

AI Self-Driving Cars
Consonance

by Dr. Lance B. Eliot, MBA, PhD

Chapter Title

This title is available via Amazon and other book sellers

ABOUT THE AUTHOR

Dr. Lance B. Eliot, Ph.D., MBA is a globally recognized AI expert and thought leader, an experienced executive and leader, a successful serial entrepreneur, and a noted scholar on AI, including that his Forbes and AI Trends columns have amassed over 2.8+ million views, his books on AI are frequently ranked in the Top 10 of all-time AI books, his journal articles are widely cited, and he has developed and fielded dozens of AI systems.

He currently serves as the CEO of Techbruim, Inc. and has over twenty years of industry experience including serving as a corporate officer in billion-dollar sized firms and was a partner in a major consulting firm. He is also a successful entrepreneur having founded, ran, and sold several high-tech related businesses.

Dr. Eliot previously hosted the popular radio show *Technotrends* that was also available on American Airlines flights via their in-flight audio program, he has made appearances on CNN, has been a frequent speaker at industry conferences, and his podcasts have been downloaded over 100,000 times.

A former professor at the University of Southern California (USC), he founded and led an innovative research lab on Artificial Intelligence. He also previously served on the faculty of the University of California Los Angeles (UCLA) and was a visiting professor at other major universities. He was elected to the International Board of the Society for Information Management (SIM), a prestigious association of over 3,000 high-tech executives worldwide.

He has performed extensive community service, including serving as Senior Science Adviser to the Congressional Vice-Chair of the Congressional Committee on Science & Technology. He has served on the Board of the OC Science & Engineering Fair (OCSEF), where he is also has been a Grand Sweepstakes judge, and likewise served as a judge for the Intel International SEF (ISEF). He served as the Vice-Chair of the Association for Computing Machinery (ACM) Chapter, a prestigious association of computer scientists. Dr. Eliot has been a shark tank judge for the USC Mark Stevens Center for Innovation on start-up pitch competitions and served as a mentor for several incubators and accelerators in Silicon Valley and in Silicon Beach.

Dr. Eliot holds a Ph.D. from USC, MBA, and Bachelor's in Computer Science, and earned the CDP, CCP, CSP, CDE, and CISA certifications.

ADDENDUM

AI Self-Driving Cars Consonance

Practical Advances in Artificial Intelligence (AI) and Machine Learning

By

Dr. Lance B. Eliot, MBA, PhD

For supplemental materials of this book, visit:

www.ai-selfdriving-cars.guru

For special orders of this book, contact:

LBE Press Publishing

Email: LBE.Press.Publishing@gmail.com

www.ingramcontent.com/pod-product-compliance
Lightning Source LLC
Chambersburg PA
CBHW051046050326
40690CB00006B/616
9781734601695